America's Best-Loved

Community Cookbook Recipes

Casual Suppers

Better Homes and Gardens.

Better Homes and Gardens® Books
Des Moines

BETTER HOMES AND GARDENS® BOOKS
An Imprint of Meredith® Books

America's Best-Loved Community Cookbook Recipes
Casual Suppers
Editor: Christopher Cavanaugh
Copy Chief: Gregory H. Kayko
Associate Art Director: Tom Wegner
Designers: Terry Kopel, Jeff Harrison
Copywriter: Kim Gayton Elliott
Production Manager: Bill Rose

Director, New Product Development: Ray Wolf
Test Kitchen Director: Sharon Stilwell

Meredith Publishing Group
President, Publishing Group: Christopher Little
Vice President and Publishing Director: John P. Loughlin

Meredith Corporation
Chairman and Chief Executive Officer: Jack D. Rehm
President and Chief Operating Officer: William T. Kerr

Chairman of the Executive Committee: E.T. Meredith III

Our seal assures you that every recipe in **America's Best-Loved Community Cookbook Recipes:** *Casual Suppers* has been tested in the *Better Homes and Gardens® Test Kitchen.* This means that each recipe is practical and reliable, and meets our high standards of taste appeal. We guarantee your satisfaction with this book for as long as you own it.

casual suppers

Suppertime—and the cooking is easy! *Better Homes and Gardens*® is committed to making life simpler and better for you. In this volume of *America's Best-Loved Community Cookbook Recipes: Casual Suppers,* we offer a sensational selection of mouth-watering meals that don't strain the cook.

Because almost every recipe in *Casual Suppers* is a one-dish wonder, you need only add a simple salad and some French bread for a complete meal. Meat-fanciers will delight in satisfying Shepherd's Pie or Vegetable and Meatball Soup. Classic Chicken 'N Dumplings and Turkey Marengo are two of the prize poultry recipes; meatless marvels include Pasta Nests and Vegetables and Parmesan Corn Chowder. Seafood dishes such as Bob Burn's Bouillabaisse and Deep Dish Salmon Pie bring the treaures of the sea to your table. Plus, every recipe has passed the *Better Homes and Gardens*® *Test Kitchen* and has earned the *Better Homes and Gardens*® *Test Kitchen Seal of Approval.* You'll find time-smart tips, cooking savvy, and creative serving suggestions to help you get the most out of your kitchen.

You'll also find wonderful stories about these delectable dishes from the cooks themselves—family favorites handed down through the generations, "secret" recipes shared among neighbors, and creative solutions to culinary dilemmas. For casual suppers at their very best, you just can't beat *America's Best-Loved Community Cookbook Recipes: Casual Suppers.*

contents

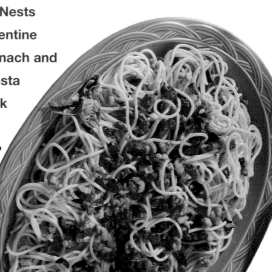

meats

For many Americans, dinner isn't dinner without some form of meat. This chapter is the answer to meat-lovers' dreams. Robust, traditional, and soul-satisfying dishes such as Shepherd's Pie, Split Pea Soup and Ham, and Beef Stew will gratify even the heartiest appetite. Celebrate the diversity of ethnic food in America, and whip up Creole Black-Eyed Peas and Rice, Rueben Casserole á la Orcas, Homemade Minestrone, or Pork and Sauerkraut Supper. Or, defy culinary convention with Pizza Popover Pie or Double Cheese and Macaroni with Ham. Dinner is well served!

PORK AND SAUERKRAUT SUPPER

PORK AND SAUERKRAUT SUPPER

Makes 6 Servings

2	tablespoons cooking oil
6	pork ribs *or* loin chops, each cut ¾ inch thick (about 2¼ pounds)
1	medium onion, finely chopped (½ cup)
1¾	cups apple juice
2	16-ounce bags *or* two 14- to 16-ounce cans *or* jars sauerkraut, drained
3	medium potatoes (1 pound), cut into ¼-inch slices
2	red cooking apples, cored and cut into ½-inch chunks
2	teaspoons brown sugar
½	teaspoon salt
⅛	teaspoon pepper

♦   ♦   ♦

Although *The Breckenridge Genuine Colorado Cookbook is geared toward high-elevation cooking (Breckenridge is 10,000 feet above sea level), Debra Edwards, executive director of the foundation, emphasizes that these terrific recipes have been adapted to work at any elevation.*

Chris Wilson
Breckenridge Genuine Colorado Cookbook
Summit Foundation
Breckenridge
COLORADO

1 Heat the oil in a 12-inch skillet over medium-high heat. Add the pork chops and brown on both sides. Remove the pork chops and set aside.

2 Preheat the oven to 350°.

3 In the drippings remaining in skillet, cook and stir the onion over medium heat until tender. Carefully add *¼ cup* apple juice, stirring to loosen the browned bits from the bottom of the skillet. Transfer the mixture to a 13x9x2-inch baking dish.

4 In the baking dish, stir together the onion mixture, drained sauerkraut, sliced potatoes, apple chunks, brown sugar and the remaining apple juice.

5 Tuck the pork chops in the sauerkraut mixture and sprinkle with the salt and pepper. Cover the baking dish with foil and bake in the 350° oven about 2 hours or until the meat and potatoes are tender. During baking, occasionally lift the foil and baste the pork chops and potatoes with the liquid in the baking dish.

 TIPS FROM OUR KITCHEN

To save time and to give the dish more color, leave the peels on the potatoes and apples.

Sauerkraut is made by allowing shredded cabbage to ferment for several weeks in a brine of cabbage juice and salt. Sauerkraut flavors vary somewhat depending on the brand used. To use, place sauerkraut in a sieve and drain well before adding it to other ingredients. To reduce the salty, strong flavor, rinse the sauerkraut under cold, running water.

Nutrition Analysis: (*Per Serving*): Calories: 401 / Cholesterol: 79 mg / Carbohydrates: 36 g / Protein: 26 g / Sodium: 759 mg / Fat: 18 g (Saturated Fat: 5 g) / Potassium: 937 mg.

VEAL OVEN STEW

Makes 6 Servings

3	tablespoons all-purpose flour
2	pounds veal leg round roast, cut into 1½-inch cubes
3	tablespoons cooking oil
12	small white onions, peeled
12	small carrots, peeled and cut into 1-inch pieces *or* one 10-ounce package frozen baby carrots
12	ounces fresh mushrooms, trimmed
2	tablespoons all-purpose flour
3	tablespoons prepared mustard
½	teaspoon salt
1½	cups dry white wine
1	cup tomato juice
	Hot cooked wide egg noodles (optional)

◆   ◆   ◆

James W. Roemer, Jr. got this recipe from his grandmother, who recently celebrated her 90th birthday. She was given the recipe by her mother. James says, "You can make this dish in advance and entertain your guests while dinner is in the oven."

James W. Roemer, Jr.
<u>*Capital Connoisseur*</u>
Lawrence Center Independence
House
Schenectady
NEW YORK

1 Preheat the oven to 350°

2 Place the 3 tablespoons flour in a plastic bag. Add a few cubes of the veal at a time, and shake to coat with the flour. Repeat with the remaining veal.

3 In a large skillet over medium-high heat, brown the meat in the cooking oil. Remove the meat and transfer to a 3-quart round casserole. Add the onions, carrots and mushrooms to the casserole.

4 Add the 2 tablespoons flour, the mustard and salt to the hot oil in the skillet; stir to make a paste.

5 Add the wine and tomato juice to the skillet. Cook and stir until the gravy is slightly thickened. Pour the gravy over the meat and vegetables in the casserole.

6 Cover the casserole and bake in the 350° oven about 1½ hours or until the meat and vegetables are tender. If the gravy becomes too thick, add a small amount of water or wine. If desired, serve over hot cooked noodles.

 TIPS FROM OUR KITCHEN

Coating the meat cubes with flour gives them a rich brown color when cooked. To ensure that the meat cubes brown evenly, add only half of the meat to the skillet at a time.

If small onions aren't available, cut a whole, large onion into 12 wedges.

Nutrition Analysis (*Per Serving*): Calories: 388 / Cholesterol: 123 mg / Carbohydrates: 20 g / Protein: 37 g / Sodium: 541 mg / Fat: 13 g (Saturated Fat: 4 g) / Potassium: 1027 mg.

VEAL OVEN STEW

SHEPHERD'S PIE

SHEPHERD'S PIE

Makes 8 Servings

1 pound ground beef
1 pound bulk pork sausage
1 medium onion, chopped (½ cup)
1 clove garlic, minced
1 16-ounce bag frozen mixed vegetables, thawed
1 15-ounce can tomato sauce
1 tablespoon Worcestershire sauce
6 medium potatoes (2 pounds)
¼ cup margarine *or* butter
2 tablespoons milk
¼ teaspoon salt
⅛ teaspoon pepper

♦   ♦   ♦

Tom Rowe really enjoys experimenting and creating his own recipes. About 25 years ago, when Tom was in the Coast Guard, the cook made a dish that was very similar to Shepherd's Pie. Tom liked it so much that he made up his own recipe, working backwards and adding different ingredients until his Shepherd's Pie was just right.

Tom Rowe
Treasured Recipes
Ketchikan Volunteer Fire Department
Ketchikan
ALASKA

1 Preheat the oven to 350°.

2 In a 12-inch skillet over medium-high heat, cook the beef, pork sausage, onion and garlic until the beef and pork sausage are browned and the onion is tender; drain off fat. Transfer the beef and pork sausage mixture to a 3-quart round casserole.

3 Add the vegetables, tomato sauce and Worcestershire sauce to the beef and pork sausage in the casserole dish; stir to mix. Cover and bake in the 350° oven for 45 minutes.

4 Meanwhile, peel the potatoes; cut into quarters. Place the potatoes in a large saucepan in enough *water* to cover; bring to a boil. Reduce heat; cover and simmer for 20 to 25 minutes or until the potatoes are very tender; drain.

5 In a large mixing bowl using an electric mixer or a potato masher, mash the cooked potatoes. Add the margarine or butter and milk; beat until stiff. Season with the salt and pepper.

6 Stir the hot beef and pork sausage mixture. Dollop the mashed potatoes on top. Bake, uncovered, for 30 minutes more.

 TIPS FROM OUR KITCHEN

If desired, you can substitute 2 cups of chopped cooked beef or pork for the ground beef in this recipe. For a spicier flavor, use hot-flavored pork sausage.

You can reduce the fat content in this recipe by using ground skinless turkey for all or part of the pork sausage.

By adding *only* 2 tablespoons of milk to the cooked potatoes, the mashed potatoes will be stiff rather than soft.

For a more colorful topping, sprinkle the potatoes with shredded cheddar cheese or paprika before serving.

Nutrition Analysis (*Per Serving*): Calories: 411 / Cholesterol: 57 mg / Carbohydrates: 35 g / Protein: 20 g / Sodium: 872 mg / Fat: 22 g (Saturated Fat: 7 g) / Potassium: 915 mg.

STUFFED BELL PEPPERS

Makes 6 Servings

- 6 medium green, red *and/or* yellow sweet peppers
- 1 pound ground beef
- 1 large onion, chopped
- ½ cup chopped green onions
- 1 clove garlic, minced
- 1 10-ounce package frozen white-and-wild rice mixture, thawed
- 1 4-ounce can sliced mushrooms, drained
- ½ cup fine dry bread crumbs
- ¼ cup butter *or* margarine, cut into pieces
- ¼ cup grated Romano *or* Parmesan cheese
- Dash dried oregano, crushed
- Dash dried basil, crushed
- 3 eggs, slightly beaten
- 6 tablespoons fine dry bread crumbs (optional)
- 1 tablespoon butter *or* margarine (optional)
- 2 slices process American cheese

◆ ◆ ◆

At one time, Jane Van Norman didn't know how to cook, so she began collecting cookbooks and taught herself. She now has well over 600 cookbooks, some dating back to the late 1800s.

Jane Van Norman
Bell's Best
Telephone Pioneers of America
Mississippi Chapter No. 36
Jackson
MISSISSIPPI

1 Preheat the oven to 350°.

2 Cut off the tops of the sweet peppers. Carefully remove and discard the membranes and seeds from inside each sweet pepper. Place the sweet peppers right side up in a large saucepan. Fill the saucepan with enough *cold water* to cover the sweet peppers. Bring the water to a boil; boil for 3 to 4 minutes or until the sweet peppers are just tender. Using tongs, carefully invert and place the sweet peppers on paper towels to drain.

3 In a large skillet over medium heat, cook the ground beef, onion, green onions and garlic until the beef is no longer pink. Drain; discard the fat.

4 Add the rice, mushrooms, the ½ cup bread crumbs, the ¼ cup butter or margarine, the Romano or Parmesan cheese, oregano, basil and ¼ teaspoon *pepper* to the beef mixture, stirring to mix the ingredients and to melt the butter or margarine. Remove the skillet from the heat and stir in the slightly beaten eggs. Return the skillet to very low heat and cook for 5 minutes.

5 Place the sweet peppers, right side up, in a 13x9x2-inch baking dish. Spoon the stuffing mixture into the sweet peppers, dividing the mixture equally. Sprinkle *1 tablespoon* of the bread crumbs and a dot of butter or margarine over *each* stuffed sweet pepper, if desired.

6 Bake the stuffed sweet peppers in the 350° oven for 15 minutes. Cut cheese into strips. Place 2 strips crisscross on top of each pepper. Return the dish to the oven just until the cheese melts.

 TIPS FROM OUR KITCHEN

One large onion will yield about 1 cup of chopped onion called for in this recipe. For the ½ cup of chopped green onions, you'll need 4 green onions.

You'll need about 3½ slices of dried bread to make the bread crumbs used in the filling and topping. Use a food processor or place the dried bread in a heavy plastic bag and crush the bread with a rolling pin.

Nutrition Analysis (*Per Serving*): Calories: 430 / Cholesterol: 187 mg / Carbohydrates: 26 g / Protein: 24 g / Sodium: 711 mg / Fat: 26 g (Saturated Fat: 12 g) / Potassium: 662 mg.

STUFFED BELL PEPPERS

15

EGGPLANT CASSEROLE

EGGPLANT CASSEROLE

Makes 6 to 7 Servings

1   pound ground beef
1   cup chopped onion
½   cup tomato paste
½   cup water
2   tablespoons margarine *or* butter
2   tablespoons snipped parsley
½   teaspoon salt
⅛   teaspoon pepper
⅓   cup fine dry bread crumbs
2   medium eggplants (about 1 pound each)
⅓   cup all-purpose flour
¼   cup olive oil
2   eggs, well beaten
¼   cup grated Parmesan cheese

◆   ◆   ◆

When Maria Dionyssopoulas's daughter gets married, Maria will be passing along her collection of recipes, including this one for Moussaka, which she received from her in-laws in Greece. Maria tells us that she sometimes leaves out the ground beef for a meatless version of this family-favorite dish.

Maria Dionyssopoulas
Grecian Delights
The Ladies of the Philoptochos of the Virgin Mary Greek Orthodox Church
Plymouth
MICHIGAN

1 Preheat the oven to 350°. Grease a 2-quart rectangular baking dish. Set aside.

2 In a large skillet, cook the beef and onion until browned. Drain the fat from the meat mixture. Add the tomato paste, water, margarine or butter, parsley, salt and pepper. Bring the mixture to a boil; reduce the heat and simmer, uncovered, for 1 minute. Stir in *2 tablespoons* of the bread crumbs.

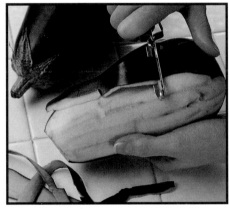

3 Using a vegetable peeler, peel the eggplants. Slice them crosswise into ¼-inch-thick slices. Coat each slice lightly with the flour. In a large skillet, cook the eggplant slices in the olive oil until golden brown on both sides. Add more oil to the skillet as necessary.

4 Sprinkle the prepared baking dish with *2 tablespoons* of the bread crumbs. Arrange *half* of the eggplant slices in the baking dish. Top with half of the meat sauce. Repeat with the remaining eggplant and meat sauce. Pour the beaten eggs over the top. Combine the Parmesan cheese and the remaining bread crumbs and sprinkle the mixture over the top of the casserole. Bake in the 350° oven for 25 to 30 minutes or until heated through.

   TIPS FROM OUR KITCHEN

Western eggplant is the most common variety in the United States. It is large and usually pear-shaped—although it can be round—with a smooth, glossy, purple or white skin. White eggplant is smaller and firmer with a tougher, thicker skin and slightly sweeter flesh. Japanese eggplant is long, slender and purple with a mild flavor.

When shopping, choose eggplants that are plump, glossy and heavy for their size. Caps should be fresh-looking, tight and mold-free. Store eggplants in the refrigerator up to two days.

Nutrition Analysis (*Per Serving*): Calories: 398 / Cholesterol: 122 mg / Carbohydrates: 26 g / Protein: 21 g / Sodium: 411 mg / Fat: 24 g (Saturated Fat: 6 g) / Potassium: 804 mg.

Makes 6 to 8 Servings

- 8 ounces wide noodles, cooked and drained
- 3 tablespoons butter *or* margarine, softened
- 1 pound sauerkraut, drained
- 2 cups chopped corned beef
- 2 medium tomatoes, peeled and sliced
- ¼ cup Thousand Island salad dressing
- 2 cups shredded Swiss cheese (8 ounces)
- 4 crisp rye crackers, crushed
- ½ teaspoon caraway seed

❖ ❖ ❖

Patricia Jorgensen and her family love to ski—and they love Reuben sandwiches—so whenever they embark on a ski trip, Patricia is sure to bring along her Reuben Casserole. It is a quick, tasty winter dish that is perfect for those cozy dinners in the ski cabin. Patricia tells us that she frequently serves this casserole to dinner guests at home as well.

Patricia Jorgensen
Orcas Cuisine
Orcas Island Medical Guild
Eastsound
Orcas Island
WASHINGTON

1 Preheat the oven to 350°. Grease a 2-quart baking dish. Set aside.

2 While the noodles are still hot, place them in a bowl. Add the butter or margarine and stir to coat.

3 Layer the buttered noodles, sauerkraut, corned beef and tomatoes in the prepared baking dish. Dot with the Thousand Island salad dressing and sprinkle with the cheese.

4 Top the casserole with the crushed cracker crumbs and the caraway seed.

5 Bake, covered, in the 350° oven for 40 minutes. Uncover and bake for 15 minutes more or until bubbly.

TIPS FROM OUR KITCHEN

For easier serving, stir together the noodles, sauerkraut and *half* of the cheese before placing it in the baking dish. Layer the corned beef, tomato slices and Thousand Island salad dressing, then sprinkle the remaining cheese on top.

You may want to substitute caraway cheese for the Swiss cheese and caraway seed.

Corned beef is a beef product usually made from fresh beef brisket or beef round and cured with spices added to a salt brine. Corned beef tastes slightly salty and has a deep red color. You'll find ready-to-cook corned beef in the meat case.

An easy way to crush crackers is to place them inside a heavy plastic bag and then roll a rolling pin over them.

Nutrition Analysis (*Per Serving*): Calories: 530 / Cholesterol: 103 mg / Carbohydrates: 38 g / Protein: 26 g / Sodium: 1221 mg / Fat: 30 g (Saturated Fat: 14 g) / Potassium: 375 mg.

RUEBEN CASSEROLE Á LA ORCAS

YANKEE NOODLE DANDY

YANKEE NOODLE DANDY

Makes 8 to 10 Servings
- 1 pound ground beef
- 1 clove garlic, minced
- ¼ teaspoon pepper
- 1 1½-ounce envelope spaghetti sauce mix
- 3 cups water
- 1 6-ounce can tomato paste
- ½ teaspoon dried thyme, crushed
- 1 8-ounce package medium *or* wide noodles, cooked and drained (4 cups)
- 1 cup dairy sour cream
- 1 3-ounce package cream cheese, softened
- ½ cup grated Parmesan cheese
- 1 tablespoon snipped parsley

◆　◆　◆

Jinny Merrill and Teddy Geokezas were both in the same sorority and about 20 years ago, they helped their younger sorority sisters during rush week. One way Jinny and Teddy helped out was by bringing food, and for one dinner Teddy brought Noodles Riviera (also called Yankee Noodle Dandy). Jinny requested the recipe, and she's made it for friends and family ever since.

Jinny Merrill
10,000 Tastes of Minnesota
The Women's Club of Minneapolis
Minneapolis
MINNESOTA

1 In a large skillet, cook and stir the ground beef and garlic until the beef is brown. Drain the fat from the skillet. Stir in the pepper.

2 In a small bowl, stir together the spaghetti sauce mix, water, tomato paste and thyme. Stir the spaghetti sauce mixture into the beef mixture. Bring the mixture to a boil. Reduce heat and simmer the meat sauce for 20 minutes.

3 Preheat the oven to 325°. Place *half* of the cooked noodles in a 3-quart rectangular baking dish. Spread *half* of the meat sauce over the noodles.

4 In another small bowl, stir together the sour cream, cream cheese, ¼ *cup* of the Parmesan cheese and the parsley. Spread *two-thirds* of the cheese mixture over the meat-sauce layer in the baking dish.

5 Spread the remaining noodles over the cheese layer. Completely cover the top layer of noodles with the remaining meat sauce. Spread the remaining cheese mixture in the center of the casserole. Sprinkle the remaining Parmesan cheese over all.

6 Bake in the 325° oven about 20 minutes or until the casserole is heated through.

 TIPS FROM OUR KITCHEN

If desired, use ground turkey or Italian sausage for half of the ground beef.

Avoid overcooking the noodles since they're going into a baked casserole.

For a change, substitute spinach noodles for part of the 8 ounces of regular noodles.

Store any leftovers in individual microwave-safe containers for next-day lunches.

Nutrition Analysis (*Per Serving*): Calories: 369 / Cholesterol: 89 mg / Carbohydrates: 28 g / Protein: 19 g / Sodium: 816 mg / Fat: 20 g (Saturated Fat: 11 g) / Potassium: 451 mg.

VEGETABLE AND MEATBALL SOUP

Makes 6 to 8 Servings

1	16-ounce can tomatoes, cut up
3	medium potatoes, peeled and cubed
1	cup sliced carrots
¾	cup chopped celery
1	medium onion, chopped
1	bay leaf
1	tablespoon snipped parsley
2	teaspoons sugar
2	teaspoons instant beef bouillon granules
1½	teaspoons dried basil, crushed
1	teaspoon dried oregano, crushed
½	teaspoon seasoned pepper
¼	teaspoon salt
1	pound ground beef *or* ground turkey
1	egg
3	tablespoons finely crushed saltine crackers
1	tablespoon milk
1	teaspoon seasoned salt
1	16-ounce can cut green beans, drained
1	8-ounce can whole kernel corn, drained

❖   ❖   ❖

Virginia Iten often makes enough of this soup to keep over the winter because it freezes so well.

Virginia Iten
Kitchen Harmony
The Mid-Columbia Symphony
Guild
Richland
WASHINGTON

1 In a Dutch oven, stir together 3 cups *water*, the *undrained* tomatoes, potatoes, carrots, celery, onion, bay leaf, parsley, sugar, beef bouillon granules, basil, oregano, seasoned pepper and salt. Bring the mixture to a boil.

2 Meanwhile, in a large bowl, stir together the ground beef or turkey, egg, crushed crackers, milk, seasoned salt and a dash *pepper*; mix well. Shape the meat mixture into 1-inch balls.

3 Carefully drop the meatballs, one at a time, into the boiling soup. Reduce heat; cover and simmer the soup for 30 minutes.

4 Add the green beans and corn to the soup; cook until heated through.

 TIPS FROM OUR KITCHEN

When making the meatballs, use lean ground beef because they are cooked directly in the soup. Or, use ground turkey made with a minimum amount of skin.

Shaping the meatballs can take a little time. If you want to speed things up, drop the meat mixture by spoonfuls into the broth; although faster, the meatballs will not be as round.

To substitute fresh herbs for the dried herbs in this recipe, use 4 teaspoons of fresh basil and 1 tablespoon of fresh oregano.

Frozen mixed vegetables can be used instead of canned vegetables in this recipe.

Nutrition Analysis (*Per Serving*): Calories: 388 / Cholesterol: 83 mg / Carbohydrates: 49 g / Protein: 21 g / Sodium: 946 mg / Fat: 13 g (Saturated Fat: 5 g) / Potassium: 864 mg.

VEGETABLE AND MEATBALL SOUP

23

PIZZA POPOVER PIE

PIZZA POPOVER PIE

♦   ♦   ♦

The North Iowa Girl Scout Council put together Prairie Potpourri to raise funds in part to "assure the future of Girl Scouting in the area." Recipes were contributed by local Girl Scouts, adult volunteers and friends. This delicious recipe for Pizza Popover Pie was submitted by Tisha May, a former Girl Scout and current Girl Scout Leader.

Tisha May
Prairie Potpourri
North Iowa Girl Scout Council
Mason City
IOWA

1 Preheat the oven to 400°.

2 In a 12-inch skillet, cook and stir the ground beef, green sweet pepper and onion until the meat is browned. Drain.

3 Add the tomato sauce, spaghetti sauce mix, water, garlic powder (if using) and oregano to the meat mixture in the skillet. Mix well. Bring the mixture to a boil. Remove from heat.

4 Immediately spoon the sauce mixture into a 3-quart round casserole. Sprinkle with the mozzarella cheese.

5 In a medium mixing bowl, stir together the flour, milk, eggs and cooking oil; mix well. Transfer the batter to a glass measuring cup. Carefully pour the popover batter over the mozzarella cheese in the casserole. Sprinkle with the Parmesan cheese. Bake in the 400° oven about 25 minutes or until light brown and set.

TIPS FROM OUR KITCHEN

You can convert this dish into a Mexican "pizza" by substituting taco seasoning mix for the spaghetti sauce mix, and cheddar or Monterey Jack cheese for the mozzarella cheese.

If desired, substitute ground pork, turkey or chicken for all or part of the ground beef.

If possible, avoid interruptions when assembling this dish. It's important that the meat be hot when pouring on the batter so it will "puff" as desired. The high baking temperature also contributes to the puffing.

Use large eggs, not small or medium, to give the puffy topping the volume it needs.

Nutrition Analysis (*Per Serving*): Calories: 529 / Cholesterol: 170 mg / Carbohydrates: 32 g / Protein: 40 g / Sodium: 1410 mg / Fat: 27 g (Saturated Fat: 12 g) / Potassium: 802 mg.

Makes 8 to 10 Servings

Pizza Dough:

2¾ to 3¼	cups bread flour *or* all-purpose flour
1	package active dry yeast
¼	teaspoon salt
1	cup warm water (120° to 130°)
2	tablespoons cooking oil
	Cornmeal

Sauce:

1	pound bulk Italian sausage
1	14½-ounce can Italian-style plum tomatoes, cut up
1	cup water
¼	cup tomato paste
2	teaspoons dried oregano, crushed
2	teaspoons dried thyme, crushed
2	teaspoons dried basil, crushed
1	clove garlic, minced
½	cup sliced fresh mushrooms
½	medium onion, sliced and separated into rings
1	tablespoon olive oil
2	cups shredded mozzarella, Swiss, *and/or* cheddar cheese

♦   ♦   ♦

The Utah Dining Car Junior League of Ogden Cookbook

The Junior League of Ogden

Ogden

UTAH

1 To make the pizza dough: In a large mixing bowl, combine *1¼ cups* of the flour, the yeast and salt. Add the warm water and cooking oil. Beat with an electric mixer on low speed for 30 seconds, scraping the sides of the bowl constantly. Beat on high speed for 3 minutes, continuing to scrape the bowl. Using a wooden spoon, stir in as much of the remaining flour as you can.

2 On a lightly floured surface, knead the dough for 6 to 8 minutes, adding enough of the remaining flour to make a moderately stiff dough that is smooth and elastic. Cover the dough and let rest for 10 minutes.

3 Preheat the oven to 375°. Grease a 12-inch cast iron skillet or deep-dish pizza pan; sprinkle with the cornmeal. With greased fingers, pat the dough into the bottom and halfway up the side of the prepared pan; cover and let rise in a warm place for 30 to 45 minutes or until nearly doubled in size. Bake in the 375° oven for 20 to 25 minutes or until lightly browned.

4 Meanwhile, to prepare the sauce: In a large skillet, brown the sausage. Drain and discard any fat. Add the *undrained* tomatoes, water, tomato paste, oregano, thyme, basil and garlic to the sausage. Bring to a boil; reduce heat. Cover and simmer about 12 minutes or until the sauce has thickened. Spread the sauce over the prebaked crust.

5 In a medium bowl, toss together the sliced mushrooms, onion rings and olive oil. Sprinkle the mixture over the top of the pizza. Top with the mozzarella, Swiss and/or cheddar cheese. Bake for 15 to 20 minutes more or until the topping is bubbly. Let the pizza stand for 5 to 10 minutes before cutting into wedges.

♦   ♦   ♦

 TIPS FROM OUR KITCHEN

If you like, there are several meats you can substitute for the Italian sausage: pork sausage; turkey sausage; ground beef, pork or turkey; chopped ham; Canadian bacon; or pepperoni.

Prebaking the crust helps prevent it from becoming soggy under this saucy filling.

Nutrition Analysis (*Per Serving*): Calories: 449 / Cholesterol: 48 mg / Carbohydrates: 41 g / Protein: 22 g / Sodium: 676 mg / Fat: 21 g (Saturated Fat: 8 g) / Potassium: 448 mg.

CHICAGO PIZZA

FRIED RICE

Makes 4 to 6 Servings
2 tablespoons cooking oil
1 cup diced barbecued pork *or* leftover cooked pork *or* ham
¼ cup sliced green onion
4 cups cold, cooked long grain rice
½ cup frozen peas, thawed
½ cup chopped celery
2 tablespoons soy sauce
2 eggs, lightly beaten
Toasted sesame oil
Pepper
Onion brushes (optional)

❖ ❖ ❖

Gilroy Chow comes from a large Chinese family (six children) and rice was served at every meal. This recipe for Fried Rice was his mother's, and Gilroy believes that she probably used it back in the 1940s. This dish is easy to make and lends itself to quick cleanup: you simply add one ingredient after another to a wok, stir-fry for a few minutes, toss and serve. Gilroy suggested substituting beef or chicken for the pork.

Gilroy Chow
Family Secrets...the Best of the Delta
Lee Academy
Clarksdale
MISSISSIPPI

1 Pour cooking oil into a nonstick wok or large heavy skillet. Preheat over medium-high heat. Add the pork or ham and green onion; stir-fry for 1 minute.

2 Add the cooked rice, peas, celery and soy sauce. Cook for 3 to 5 minutes or until the mixture is heated through, tossing gently to coat all of the ingredients with the soy sauce. Push the rice mixture to the sides of the wok.

3 Add the lightly beaten eggs to the center of the wok or skillet. Cook and stir about 1 minute or until the eggs are completely cooked and well mixed with the other ingredients. Add several drops of the toasted sesame oil and pepper to taste. Stir until the ingredients are well mixed and serve immediately. If desired, garnish with onion brushes.

 TIPS FROM OUR KITCHEN

Barbecued pork can be purchased at an Asian deli or restaurant. Or, you can use cooked pork mixed with about 2 tablespoons of your favorite barbecue sauce or an oriental-flavored barbecue sauce.

The consistency of rice varies depending on the type of rice and the amount of water used. If you enjoy using chop sticks with Chinese food, sticky rice is much easier to pick up. However, if you prefer rice that is drier, less sticky and retains individual grains, use long grain rice rather than medium or short grain rice. Measure the water carefully and err on the side of too little rather than too much.

You can substitute low-sodium soy sauce for the regular soy sauce in this recipe.

Stir the pork or ham and rice during cooking to help prevent the mixture from sticking to the wok or skillet.

Nutrition Analysis (*Per Serving*): Calories: 477 / Cholesterol: 141 mg / Carbohydrates: 62 g / Protein: 21 g / Sodium: 609 mg / Fat: 15 g (Saturated Fat: 4 g) / Potassium: 357 mg.

DOUBLE CHEESE AND MACARONI WITH HAM

Makes 6 Servings

1   cup elbow macaroni
1   tablespoon margarine *or* butter
1½ cups milk
3   eggs, beaten
1   cup soft bread crumbs
1   cup shredded cheddar cheese (4 ounces)
½   cup shredded Swiss cheese (2 ounces)
½   cup julienne strips of ham (2½ ounces)
1   teaspoon dried minced onion
1   teaspoon dried parsley flakes
2   teaspoons margarine *or* butter, melted
Paprika (optional)
Green pepper slices (optional)

◆   ◆   ◆

Barbara Harms first tasted this dish 15 years ago at a Girl Scout potluck dinner. She liked the dish so much that she waited to find out who made it and to get the recipe—they've been friends ever since. Barbara says that although it would be an easy recipe to alter, there's no need to because it's "fantastic just the way it is!"

Barbara Harms
Cooking with Nostalgia II
The South Holland Historical Society
South Holland
ILLINOIS

1 Preheat the oven to 325°. Lightly grease a 2-quart square baking dish; set aside.

2 In a large saucepan, cook the macaroni in boiling *salted water* according to the package directions; drain well. Return the macaroni to the saucepan and add the 1 tablespoon margarine or butter. Stir until the margarine or butter is melted.

3 Add the milk, beaten eggs, *¾ cup* of the bread crumbs, the cheddar cheese, Swiss cheese, ham strips, onion, parsley, ¼ teaspoon *salt* and ⅛ teaspoon *pepper*. Stir until all of the ingredients are well mixed.

4 Pour the macaroni mixture into the prepared baking dish. Toss the remaining bread crumbs with the 2 teaspoons melted margarine or butter. Sprinkle the bread crumb mixture over the top of the casserole. If desired, sprinkle with the paprika.

5 Bake in the 325° oven about 35 minutes or until the casserole is heated through; the mixture will appear set in the center.

6 Garnish with slices of green pepper, if desired, and serve immediately.

TIPS FROM OUR KITCHEN

Try other pasta shapes in this recipe such as wagon wheels (upper left), corkscrews (upper right), ruffles (lower left) or bow ties (lower right).

To yield the 1 cup of soft bread crumbs you'll need about 1½ slices of bread. To make the crumbs, freeze the bread slices and then use a shredder to make the crumbs. Or, tear leftover bread heels and place them in a blender container or a food processor bowl. Blend or process until the bread forms fine crumbs. Store the bread crumbs in an airtight container in the freezer.

Nutrition Analysis (*Per Serving*): Calories: 319 / Cholesterol: 146 mg / Carbohydrates: 22 g / Protein: 19 g / Sodium: 524 mg / Fat: 17 g (Saturated Fat: 8 g) / Potassium: 221 mg.

Double Cheese and Macaroni with Ham

RED BEANS AND RICE

RED BEANS AND RICE

Makes 8 Servings

1	meaty ham bone *or* ham hocks (1 to 1½ pounds)
1	pound dry red kidney beans
1	teaspoon Worcestershire sauce
½	teaspoon garlic salt
¼	teaspoon bottled hot pepper sauce
1	cup chopped celery
1	cup chopped onion
8	ounces fully cooked smoked sausage links, sliced
4	ounces bulk hot-style pork sausage
1½	teaspoons minced garlic
2	bay leaves
¼	cup snipped parsley

Hot cooked rice

◆   ◆   ◆

According to Cookbook Chairperson Tricia Haney, The Fort Leavenworth Officers and Civilians Wives' Club originally printed The Fort Leavenworth Collection in 1983. Then in 1990, they followed up with The Fort Leavenworth Recollection. Profits from both cookbooks were used to support the club's many community activities.

Pamela Sulka
The Fort Leavenworth
Recollection
The Fort Leavenworth Officers and Civilians Wives' Club
Fort Leavenworth
KANSAS

1 In a 4-quart Dutch oven, stir together the ham bone or ham hocks, dry red beans, 11 cups *water*, Worcestershire sauce, garlic salt and hot pepper sauce. Bring the mixture to a boil; reduce heat. Cover and simmer over low heat about 3 hours or until the red beans are tender.

2 Transfer the ham bone or ham hocks to a cutting board. Cut the ham meat off the bones; discard the bones. Chop the ham; set aside.

3 In a large skillet over medium heat, cook the celery, onion, smoked sausage, hot-style sausage and minced garlic for 10 to 15 minutes or until the sausages are slightly browned and the vegetables are tender; drain off the fat.

4 Add the sausage mixture, bay leaves and ¼ teaspoon *pepper* to the red bean mixture. Simmer, uncovered, about 30 minutes or until a thick gravy forms. Remove and discard the bay leaves. Stir in the chopped ham and parsley; heat through. Serve the red bean mixture over the hot cooked rice.

TIPS FROM OUR KITCHEN

Before cooking the red kidney beans, place them in a sieve and rinse them under cold running water.

To reduce the cooking time of this dish, soak the red kidney beans in cold water overnight in a covered pan; then drain and rinse. In a Dutch oven, stir together the beans, ham bone, *half* of the water and seasonings. Cook about 1½ hours or until the beans are nearly tender; then continue as directed.

Prepare 6 cups of cooked rice to have enough cooked rice for 8 servings. To make 6 cups of cooked rice, start with 2 cups *brown* or *long grain white rice* and 4 cups *water*. Simmer the brown rice for 35 minutes or the white rice for 15 minutes. Or, use 3 cups *quick-cooking rice* and 3 cups *water* and prepare the rice according to the package directions.

Nutrition Analysis (*Per Serving*): Calories: 464 / Cholesterol: 28 mg / Carbohydrates: 64 g / Protein: 24 g / Sodium: 707 mg / Fat: 12 g (Saturated Fat: 5 g) / Potassium: 838 mg.

CREOLE BLACK-EYED PEAS AND RICE

Makes 5 Servings

1¼	cups dried black-eyed peas
¼	pound salt pork, chopped
1	pound fully cooked smoked sausage, sliced
1½	cups chopped onion
½	cup chopped green onion
½	cup chopped green sweet pepper
½	cup snipped parsley
½	cup tomato sauce
1	clove garlic, minced
1½	teaspoons Worcestershire sauce
¼ to ½	teaspoon pepper
⅛	teaspoon dried oregano, crushed
⅛	teaspoon dried thyme, crushed

Few dashes bottled hot pepper sauce

3	cups hot cooked rice (1 cup uncooked)

♦   ♦   ♦

Sylvia Moore believes this hearty dish originated in southern Louisiana. Creole Black-Eyed Peas and Rice is a perfect dish for casual company—simply serve it with a salad and a light dessert.

Sylvia Moore

Top Rankin' Recipes

Rankin General Hospital

Auxiliary

Brandon

MISSISSIPPI

1 Rinse the black-eyed peas and place them in a 4½-quart Dutch oven. Add 4 cups cold *water*. Bring to a boil; reduce heat and simmer for 2 minutes. Remove from heat. Cover and let stand for 1 hour. Drain and rinse the peas.

2 Return the peas to the Dutch oven. Add the salt pork. Add 3 cups *water* or enough to cover the peas. Cover and simmer for 45 minutes.

3 Stir in the sausage, onion, green onion, green sweet pepper, parsley, tomato sauce, garlic, Worcestershire sauce, pepper, oregano, thyme and hot pepper sauce.

4 Bring the mixture to a boil; reduce heat and simmer, covered, over low heat for 45 minutes. Serve over the hot cooked rice.

 TIPS FROM OUR KITCHEN

Use a sharp knife to cut away the rind on the salt pork before chopping it. You can substitute chopped bacon for the salt pork in this recipe.

Black-eyed peas are small, oval and cream colored, with a black oval "eye" that has a cream-colored dot in the center. Also known as cowpeas, black-eyed peas have a mealy texture and an earthy flavor. For this recipe, if you want the peas to retain their shape, don't soak them before cooking. Do rinse them, however, by placing the peas in a sieve and holding them under running water.

One cup uncooked rice will yield 3 cups cooked rice.

This recipe is easily doubled if you need to serve a crowd.

Nutrition Analysis (*Per Serving*): Calories: 804 / Cholesterol: 71 mg / Carbohydrates: 75 g / Protein: 37 g / Sodium: 1704 mg / Fat: 39 g (Saturated Fat: 14 g) / Potassium: 1015 mg.

CREOLE BLACK-EYED PEAS AND RICE

SPLIT PEA SOUP AND HAM

SPLIT PEA SOUP AND HAM

Makes 6 to 8 Servings
1   pound dry green split peas,
     rinsed and drained
1   meaty ham bone (2 pounds)
8   cups water
2   stalks celery, thinly sliced
     (1 cup)
1   large onion, thinly sliced
1   medium carrot, thinly sliced
     (½ cup)
½   teaspoon salt
¼   teaspoon pepper

♦   ♦   ♦

*Because Jean Salley and her
husband travel a lot and eat out
often, she hasn't made her Split
Pea Soup and Ham in quite
awhile. But after we called to ask
about the recipe, she remembered
how good this soup was. Jean
said, "I'm going to start making it
again." She found this to be an
excellent soup for cold weather
and said, "It's very filling; some
bread and a salad are all you'll
need to complete the meal."*

Jean Salley
<u>Kitchen Keys</u>
*The Episcopal Church Women's
Organization of St. Peter's Parish
Church
New Kent
VIRGINIA*

1 In a large saucepan or Dutch oven, stir together the split peas, ham bone, water, celery, onion, carrot, salt and pepper. Bring to a boil; reduce heat and simmer, covered, for 1 hour.

2 Remove the ham bone from the soup mixture. When it is cool enough to handle, cut the ham off the bone. Discard the bone. Coarsely chop the ham.

3 Add the ham to the soup and simmer, uncovered, for 20 to 30 minutes more or until the liquid is slightly thickened and the peas are tender. To serve, ladle the soup into individual soup bowls.

 TIPS FROM OUR KITCHEN

Dried split peas can be stored in a covered container at room temperature up to 1 year. Before cooking them, place the desired amount of peas in a wire mesh strainer and rinse thoroughly. You'll need about 2½ cups to yield 1 pound.

If desired, use 2 pounds of ham hocks instead of a ham bone. You can also substitute yellow split peas for the green split peas.

If desired, garnish each serving with a dollop of dairy sour cream.

Chill leftover soup in single-serving, microwave-safe containers for next-day lunches. If chilling the whole amount for later reheating, store in 2 small containers instead of 1 large container because the soup will chill faster in smaller quantities.

Nutrition Analysis (*Per Serving*): Calories: 321 / Cholesterol: 13 mg / Carbohydrates: 50 g / Protein: 21 g / Sodium: 2963 mg / Fat: 5 g (Saturated Fat: 2 g) / Potassium: 671 mg.

KALE SOUP

Makes 6 Servings

3	slices bacon, cut up
4	large onions, sliced (6 cups)
6	cups water
8	cups washed, trimmed and cut up kale (approximately 8 ounces)
8	ounces linguisa sausage *or* kielbasa, thinly sliced
4	cups finely chopped potatoes (1½ pounds)
1	15½-ounce can kidney beans
1	teaspoon vinegar
½	teaspoon salt
¼	teaspoon pepper

Dash of bottled hot pepper sauce

◆ ◆ ◆

When Meredith De La Vergne's father, Charles, retired, he started cooking, often creating dishes from the bounty of his large garden. This recipe for Kale Soup comes from Charles's repertoire. It's a delicious, hearty soup that Meredith describes as "especially good."

Meredith De La Vergne
<u>*Recipes From Holly Hill*</u>
Holly Hill Mental
Health Services
Raleigh
NORTH CAROLINA

1 In a Dutch oven, cook the bacon and onions until the onions are tender. Add the water, kale and sausage or kielbasa. Bring the mixture to a boil and reduce heat. Gently boil, covered, for 15 minutes.

2 Add the potatoes and *undrained* kidney beans. Bring to a boil. Cover and boil gently for 15 minutes more.

3 Stir in the vinegar, salt, pepper and hot pepper sauce. Cover and simmer the soup for 30 minutes.

 TIPS FROM OUR KITCHEN

Kale is most abundant in grocery stores during the winter. Look for small bunches with no yellow or limp leaves. Wash the leaves in cold water, pat dry, remove the stems and trim bruised leaves. Store kale in a paper towel-lined plastic bag in the refrigerator up to 3 days. Longer storage may cause the leaves to take on a bitter taste.

Linguisa is an uncooked, smoked sausage of Portuguese origin. It is made by coarsely grinding pork with garlic, cumin seed and cinnamon. The mixture is cured in brine before stuffing. Kielbasa is a cooked, smoked sausage also known as a Polish sausage. It is usually made from a combination of pork and beef, seasoned with coriander, garlic, marjoram, salt, pepper and sugar.

For easier preparation, use a food processor to slice the onions. Cut large onions in half vertically to fit them into a feed tube.

Leftover soup can be frozen in 2-cup containers. To reheat, transfer the frozen soup to a microwave-safe bowl and micro-cook on 70% power (medium-high) for 10 to 11 minutes, stirring occasionally.

Nutrition Analysis (*Per Serving*): Calories: 491 / Cholesterol: 34 mg / Carbohydrates: 51 g / Protein: 16 g / Sodium: 733 mg / Fat: 27 g (Saturated Fat: 6 g) / Potassium: 1016 mg.

KALE SOUP

BEAN SOUP WITH PASTA

BEAN SOUP WITH PASTA

Makes 4 to 6 Servings

- 1 cup dry Great Northern beans, rinsed
- 1 tablespoon olive oil
- 8 ounces fully cooked ham, cut into ¼-inch cubes (about 1½ cups)
- 1 medium onion, finely chopped (½ cup)
- ¼ cup finely chopped celery
- 1 large clove garlic, minced
- 1 4-ounce piece salt pork (optional)
- ¼ teaspoon freshly ground pepper
- 1½ ounces spaghetti, broken into 1-inch pieces (½ cup)
- Salt (optional)
- Pepper (optional)
- Snipped parsley

❖ ❖ ❖

Pot Holders and Love Handles is the result of the efforts of Lynda Cabela and her friends and family. All of the profits are given to the Amyotrophic Lateral Sclerosis (Lou Gehrig's Disease) Association for research.

Lynda Cabela
Pot Holders and Love Handles
A.L.S. Association
Woodland Hills
CALIFORNIA

1 In a Dutch oven, combine the beans and 2 quarts *water*. Bring to a boil and cook, uncovered, for 2 minutes.

2 Remove from heat; cover and let stand for 1 hour. Drain the beans, rinse and drain again. Set aside.

3 In the same Dutch oven, heat the olive oil over medium heat. Add the ham, onion, celery and garlic. Cook and stir for 5 to 10 minutes or until the onion is lightly browned.

4 Add the drained beans, 2 quarts fresh *water*, salt pork (if desired) and the ¼ teaspoon pepper. Bring to a boil; reduce heat and simmer, covered, for 1 to 1½ hours or until the beans are tender.

5 Remove and discard the salt pork, if using. Skim the fat off the soup or transfer the soup to covered containers, cool and refrigerate until the fat rises to the top and congeals. Then, lift off and discard the fat.

6 Using a slotted spoon, transfer about *half* of the beans to a mixing bowl. Mash them with a potato masher.

7 Return the mashed beans to the soup. Simmer the soup over low heat, stirring constantly, for 2 minutes. Add the broken spaghetti. Simmer the soup, covered, for 10 to 15 minutes more or until the spaghetti is tender. Taste for seasoning, adding salt or pepper, if desired. Ladle the soup into serving bowls and garnish with parsley.

TIPS FROM OUR KITCHEN

If you want a more colorful soup, add 1 cup thinly sliced carrots along with the spaghetti. Or, substitute spinach fettuccine for the spaghetti.

To make this soup easier to eat, use broken pasta instead of whole pasta.

Nutrition Analysis (*Per Serving*): Calories: 347 / Cholesterol: 30 mg / Carbohydrates: 45 g / Protein: 25 g / Sodium: 699 mg / Fat: 8 g (Saturated Fat: 2 g) / Potassium: 729 mg.

BEEF STEW

½ cup all-purpose flour
2 pounds beef stew meat, cubed
2 tablespoons shortening
1 clove garlic, minced
1 teaspoon Worcestershire sauce
2 beef bouillon cubes *or* 2 teaspoons instant beef bouillon granules
1 8-ounce can tomato sauce
1 cup chopped celery (2 stalks)
1 small onion, chopped (⅓ cup)
4 carrots, cut into 1-inch slices
3 medium potatoes, cut into eighths

◆ ◆ ◆

In 1981, the Grace Presbyterian Village Ministries established a Caring Fund to ensure support and security for its residents. Village Vittles *was created to raise a $10,000 "careship" for the fund. So far, the cookbook has raised enough money for two careships, and it is continuing to generate funds.*

Village Vittles
Grace Presbyterian Village
Auxiliary
Dallas
TEXAS

1 In a heavy plastic bag, mix together the flour, 1 teaspoon *salt* and ¼ teaspoon *pepper*. Add the beef cubes and shake to coat them completely with the flour mixture.

2 In a large skillet, melt the shortening. Add *half* the beef cubes at a time to the skillet; brown them on all sides. Return all of the beef cubes to the skillet. Add the garlic and Worcestershire sauce.

3 In a Dutch oven, stir together 6 cups *water*, the bouillon cubes or granules, tomato sauce, celery and onion; bring to a boil. Add the beef cubes. Reduce heat; cover and simmer for 1 to 1¼ hours or until the beef is nearly tender. Add the carrots and potatoes. Simmer about 30 minutes more or until the beef and vegetables are tender.

 TIPS FROM OUR KITCHEN

If desired, buy one 2½ to 3-pound chuck roast; trim the fat and cut your own beef cubes. The cubes can be cut ahead of time and refrigerated or frozen in covered containers until you are ready to make the stew.

To avoid dirtying a pan and to make cleanup easier, brown the beef cubes in the Dutch oven instead of a skillet.

If desired, add a sprig of fresh rosemary or ½ teaspoon of dried rosemary to the stew.

Nutrition Analysis (*Per Serving*): Calories: 442 / Cholesterol: 110 mg / Carbohydrates: 34 g / Protein: 40 g / Sodium: 1021 mg / Fat: 16 g (Saturated Fat: 5 g) / Potassium: 1009 mg.

BEEF STEW

HOMEMADE MINESTRONE

HOMEMADE MINESTRONE

2 tablespoons margarine *or* butter

1 pound stew beef, cut into ½- to ¾-inch cubes

7 cups water

2 15-ounce cans tomato sauce

1 14½-ounce can tomatoes, cut up

1 medium onion, chopped (½ cup)

½ cup celery, chopped

4 beef bouillon cubes, crumbled *or* 4 teaspoons instant beef bouillon granules

2 tablespoons dried parsley flakes

½ to 1 teaspoon salt

½ teaspoon dried thyme, crushed

¼ teaspoon pepper

2 cups shredded cabbage

1 cup thinly sliced zucchini

1 cup thinly sliced carrots

1 15-ounce can garbanzo beans, drained

1 cup small macaroni, uncooked

3 to 4 tablespoons grated Parmesan cheese

❖ ❖ ❖

Carol Armbrust Fey
Georgia On My Menu: A Medley
of Southern Hits
Junior League of Cobb-Marietta
Marietta
GEORGIA

1 In a 6- or 8-quart Dutch oven over medium heat, melt the margarine or butter. Add the stew beef and cook until browned. Stir in the water, tomato sauce, tomatoes, onion, celery, bouillon cubes or granules, parsley flakes, salt, thyme and pepper. Bring the mixture to a boil, then reduce the heat to low. Cover and simmer for 1 to 1¼ hours or until the beef is tender, stirring occasionally.

2 Add the cabbage, zucchini, carrots, garbanzo beans and macaroni. Return the mixture to a boil, then reduce the heat to low. Cover and simmer for 20 to 25 minutes or until the vegetables are tender and the macaroni is done, stirring occasionally.

3 Ladle the soup into bowls and top each portion with a generous sprinkling of Parmesan cheese.

 TIPS FROM OUR KITCHEN

Soups are more adaptable than many other recipes. You can give this one your individual stamp by substituting rice for the pasta or using a different pasta shape such as ditalini, anelli, bow ties, stars or broken spaghetti. Or, you might try substituting canellini, kidney or great northern beans in place of the garbanzos.

Use a plastic cutting board when cutting uncooked meat or poultry. Scrub both the cutting board and knife thoroughly with hot soapy water before using them with any other food.

You may be able to save money by cutting your own stew beef rather than buying it precut. Choose a beef chuck pot roast or a beef round steak, then ask your butcher to cut a 1-pound slice. Or, if you prefer, buy the whole piece, cut off a 1-pound slice, and use the remainder as a roast for another meal. Cut the 1-pound slice into small cubes (½- to ¾-inch) to use in this recipe. Cutting the meat into small pieces spreads the beefy flavor throughout every serving.

For a twist on the soup topper, try spooning on pesto in place of the Parmesan cheese.

Nutrition Analysis *(Per Serving)*: Calories: 305 / Cholesterol: 43 mg / Carbohydrates: 35 g / Protein: 22 g / Sodium: 1693 mg / Fat: 9 g (Saturated Fat: 3 g) / Potassium: 949 mg.

poultry

Poultry takes the prize in these phenomenal recipes, from Deluxe Chicken à la King to Buck's Eastern Carolina Brunswick Stew. Few dishes conjure a homier image than Chicken 'N Dumplings or Herbed Cream of Chicken Noodle Soup. Or, trot out the turkey, and serve your family Grandma Theresa's Turkey Soup, Turkey Potpie, or Turkey Marengo. For fun, take a savory trip around the globe with Far-Eastern inspired Chicken Stir-Fry with Vegetables and Walnuts, East Indian Mulligatawny Soup, or southern Creole Chicken Gumbo—the world never tasted so good.

CHICKEN STIR FRY WITH VEGETABLES
AND WALNUTS

CHICKEN STIR-FRY WITH VEGETABLES AND WALNUTS

Makes 4 or 5 Servings
- ½ cup water
- ¼ cup soy sauce
- 2 tablespoons dry sherry
- 4 teaspoons cornstarch
- 1 teaspoon ground ginger
- 3 tablespoons cooking oil
- ¾ cup walnuts
- 2 cloves garlic, sliced
- 8 ounces fresh mushrooms, sliced (3 cups)
- 2 whole chicken breasts, halved, skinned, boned and cut into ¾-inch pieces
- 1 medium red sweet pepper, cut into thin strips
- ½ medium green sweet pepper, cut into thin strips
- 1 bunch green onions, trimmed and sliced diagonally (½ cup)
- 2 cups fresh bean sprouts, rinsed and drained
- 2 to 2½ cups hot cooked rice

◆   ◆   ◆

Dorothy H. Lane says she loves Chicken Stir-Fry with Vegetables and Walnuts because it is a quick-to-cook, one-dish meal.

Dorothy H. Lane
Happiness is Anything Homemade
Worcester Area Association for Retarded Citizens, Inc.
Worcester
MASSACHUSETTS

1 In a small bowl, stir together the water, soy sauce, sherry, cornstarch and ginger until the cornstarch is dissolved. Set aside.

2 In a large heavy skillet or wok, heat *1 tablespoon* of the cooking oil. Add the walnuts and cook and stir over medium-low heat about 3 minutes or until the walnuts are slightly toasted. Using a slotted spoon, transfer the walnuts to a large bowl and set aside, reserving the oil in the skillet.

3 Add the garlic to the skillet. Cook and stir about 2 minutes or until the garlic is slightly browned. Remove the garlic from the skillet and discard.

4 Add *1 tablespoon* of the cooking oil to the skillet. Add the mushrooms. Cook and stir over medium-high heat for 3 to 4 minutes or until the mushrooms are lightly browned. Using a slotted spoon, transfer the mushrooms to the bowl containing the walnuts.

5 Add the remaining cooking oil to the skillet. Add the chicken. Cook and stir for 3 to 4 minutes or until the chicken is no longer pink. Using a slotted spoon, transfer the chicken to the bowl containing the walnuts and mushrooms.

6 Add the red sweet pepper, green sweet pepper and green onion to the skillet. Cook and stir about 1 minute or until the vegetables are just crisp-tender. Stir the cornstarch mixture, then add it to the skillet. Cook and stir until the mixture is thickened and bubbly. Cook and stir for 1 minute more.

7 Return the walnuts, mushrooms and chicken to the skillet. Add the bean sprouts. Stir gently to coat the mixture with the sauce; heat through. Serve with the hot cooked rice.

 TIPS FROM OUR KITCHEN

If fresh bean sprouts aren't available, you can substitute one 16-ounce can of bean sprouts. Before using, place the fresh or canned bean sprouts in a strainer and rinse under cold water.

If you use a deep skillet or wok, you will find it easier to stir and toss the foods without making a mess.

Nutrition Analysis (*Per Serving*): Calories: 530 / Cholesterol: 45 mg / Carbohydrates: 46 g / Protein: 26 g / Sodium: 1080 mg / Fat: 27 g (Saturated Fat: 4 g) / Potassium: 663 mg.

TURKEY MARENGO

Makes 4 to 6 Servings

1	tablespoon vegetable oil
2	onions, sliced and separated into rings
3	1¼- to 1½-pound turkey drumsticks, deboned and cut into pieces
2	apples, peeled, cored and chopped
1	tablespoon curry powder
¼	teaspoon salt
¼	teaspoon pepper
4	tomatoes, peeled and chopped
½	cup chicken broth
2	tablespoons lemon juice
2 to 3	cups hot cooked rice

◆   ◆   ◆

The Fontbonne Auxiliary was founded in 1947 by the Sisters of Saint Joseph of Nazareth to help support Saint John Hospital in Detroit. Today, the Auxiliary consists of nearly 1,300 people from all walks of life, who work to serve the physical, emotional and spiritual needs of the hospital community and surrounding areas.

Rosemary Zienger
Renaissance Cuisine
The Fontbonne Auxiliary
of Saint John Hospital
Detroit
MICHIGAN

1 In a 12-inch skillet, heat the oil over medium heat. Add the onions and cook until they are soft. Push the onions to the edge of the skillet.

2 Add the turkey pieces and cook and stir until the turkey is brown. Stir in the apples, curry powder, salt and pepper. Cook the mixture for 2 minutes.

3 Stir in the tomatoes, chicken broth and lemon juice until the ingredients are well mixed. Cover the skillet and simmer the mixture for 45 to 60 minutes or until the turkey is tender.

4 Uncover the skillet and boil the stew gently for 15 minutes to reduce the liquid slightly. Serve with the hot cooked rice.

 TIPS FROM OUR KITCHEN

The liquid in the stew can be a bit thin. To thicken it quickly, transfer the turkey to a serving platter and keep it warm. In a small bowl, stir together 2 tablespoons *cornstarch* and 2 tablespoons *water*. Add the cornstarch mixture to the liquid in the skillet and stir over medium heat until the sauce is slightly thickened and bubbly. Cook and stir for 2 minutes more. Serve the sauce over the turkey.

To help eliminate some of the fat from this recipe, remove the skin from the turkey legs before you cut it into pieces.

If you'd rather use thighs to make this stew, substitute two 2-2½-pound thighs for the 3 turkey drumsticks.

To bone a turkey drumstick, remove the skin so you can see the tendons. Remove the visible outer tendons using the tip of the knife to cut away.

Cut away portions of meat from the bone. To remove the long white inner tendons from the turkey pieces, pull on the end of a tendon with your fingers. At the same time, use a knife to scrape against the tendon, freeing the surrounding meat.

Nutrition Analysis (*Per Serving*): Calories: 654 / Cholesterol: 183 mg / Carbohydrates: 48 g / Protein: 67 g / Sodium: 418 mg / Fat: 20 g (Saturated Fat: 6 g) / Potassium: 1,180 mg.

TURKEY MARENGO

TORTILLA SOUP

TORTILLA SOUP

Makes 6 to 8 Servings

 2 14½-ounce cans chicken broth *or* 1 quart homemade chicken broth
 1½ to 2 cups diced, cooked, chicken
 1 medium onion, chopped
 1 4-ounce can chopped green chilies
 1 tablespoon chili powder
Dash ground red pepper
 2 cups broken corn tortilla chips
Shredded sharp cheddar cheese
 1 tomato, chopped

♦   ♦   ♦

Rosemary Mitchell likes to make Tortilla Soup in the winter, especially when she's enjoying her mountain cabin. She says that she loves the convenience and short preparation time of this recipe. Rosemary prefers using mild green chiles, but if your taste tends toward hotness, use a hotter variety.

Rosemary Mitchell
Favorite Recipes from United Methodist Church
Albuquerque
NEW MEXICO

1 In a large saucepan, stir together the chicken broth, chicken, onion, green chilies, chili powder and ground red pepper.

2 Bring the soup to boiling. Reduce heat and simmer the soup, uncovered, about 10 minutes or until the onion is tender.

3 Ladle the soup into individual bowls or a soup tureen. Add a *small handful* of the tortilla chips to each soup bowl or the entire 2 cups to the tureen. Sprinkle with the cheddar cheese and chopped tomato. Serve immediately.

 TIPS FROM OUR KITCHEN

To lower the salt in this recipe, use low-sodium chicken broth and lightly salted or no-salt tortilla chips.

For added spiciness, increase the amount of chili powder to 2 tablespoons.

If you are using homemade chicken broth in this recipe you might like to try this method for clarifying the broth. Strain your broth into a large saucepan. Stir together one *egg white* and ¼ cup *cold water*. Add to the broth and bring the mixture to boiling. Remove from heat and let stand 5 minutes. Strain the broth through a large sieve or colander lined with several layers of damp cheesecloth for cooking. Your broth will now have a crystal-clear quality.

Nutrition Analysis *(Per Serving)*: Calories: 158 / Cholesterol: 34 mg / Carbohydrates: 10 g / Protein: 15 g / Sodium: 654 mg / Fat: 6 g (Saturated Fat: 1 g) / Potassium: 341 mg.

CHICKEN 'N DUMPLINGS

Makes 6 Servings

1	3- to 3½-pound broiler-fryer chicken, cut up
2	carrots, sliced
2	stalks celery with leaves, cut up
1	medium onion, quartered
1½	teaspoons salt
¼	teaspoon pepper
8	cups water
2	tablespoons butter *or* margarine
1½	cups all-purpose flour
¼	teaspoon salt
3	tablespoons shortening
1	egg, beaten
⅓	cup water
¼	cup all-purpose flour
¼	cup water

♦ ♦ ♦

Sassafras! *was created to raise funds for the community projects sponsored by the Junior League of Springfield. The members are dedicated to various projects focusing on advocacy for children, older adults, education, the environment, the arts, health issues, socio-economic development and other women and family issues.*

Fay Ollis
Sassafras!
The Junior League of Springfield
Springfield
MISSOURI

1 In a Dutch oven, stir together the chicken, carrots, celery, onion, the 1½ teaspoons salt and the pepper. Add the 8 cups water. Bring the mixture to a boil; reduce heat. Cover and simmer for 45 minutes. Using a slotted spoon, transfer the chicken to a plate and cool slightly. Strain the broth and discard the vegetables. Return the broth to the Dutch oven. Add the butter or margarine.

2 Meanwhile, in a large bowl, stir together the 1½ cups flour and the ¼ teaspoon salt. Using a pastry blender, cut in the shortening until the mixture is crumbly. In a small bowl, mix together the beaten egg and the ⅓ cup water. Add the egg mixture all at once to the flour mixture. Stir until the ingredients are well mixed.

3 Turn out the dough onto a well-floured surface. Knead the dough for 1 to 2 minutes or until smooth. Divide the dough into *thirds*. Roll *each* third into a 10x8-inch rectangle. Allow the rectangles to dry for 20 minutes. Cut the rectangles into squares or noodles.

4 Return the broth in the Dutch oven to a boil. Gradually add the dumplings to the boiling broth. Reduce heat and simmer, uncovered, for 10 minutes.

5 Meanwhile, remove the chicken meat from the bones; discard the skin and bones. Chop the chicken meat; set aside.

6 Using a slotted spoon, remove the dumplings from the broth. Stir together the ¼ cup flour and the ¼ cup water; stir the mixture into the broth. Cook and stir until the liquid is bubbly. Return the chicken meat and dumplings to the broth and cook until heated through.

 TIPS FROM OUR KITCHEN

Cut the dough into your choice of shapes. Try squares, strips, triangles or bow ties, or use small cookie cutters for fancier shapes.

This recipe is well suited to two-step cooking. For example, you can cook the chicken one evening; then reheat the broth and add the dumplings for dinner the next night.

Serve this dish with raw or cooked vegetables. Or, if desired, add one 10-ounce package of frozen mixed vegetables to the broth.

Nutrition Analysis (*Per Serving*): Calories: 460 / Cholesterol: 125 mg / Carbohydrates: 30 g / Protein: 30 g / Sodium: 794 mg / Fat: 24 g (Saturated Fat: 8 g) / Potassium: 396 mg.

CHICKEN 'N DUMPLINGS

CREOLE CHICKEN GUMBO

CREOLE CHICKEN GUMBO

Makes 6 Main-Dish Servings

1	2½- to 3-pound broiler-fryer chicken, cut up
½	teaspoon poultry seasoning

Roux:

¼	cup cooking oil
6	tablespoons all-purpose flour
5 to 6	celery stalks, chopped (2½ cups)
1	large onion, chopped (1 cup)
1	large green sweet pepper, chopped (1 cup)
1	pound okra, sliced, *or* one 16-ounce package frozen cut okra
1	28-ounce can tomatoes, cut up
1	clove garlic, minced
½	teaspoon bottled hot pepper sauce

Hot cooked rice
Snipped parsley *or* green onion tops (optional)

♦   ♦   ♦

Ginny Puckett told us that she often used shrimp in her gumbo until she moved to an area where shrimp were not readily available. After some experimenting, Ginny created this delectable gumbo.

Ginny Puckett
Paths of Sunshine
Florida Federation of Garden Clubs, Inc.
Winter Park
FLORIDA

1 Skin the chicken, if desired; rinse and pat dry.

2 In a 4½-quart Dutch oven, stir together the chicken, 6 cups *water*, poultry seasoning and 1 teaspoon *salt*. Bring the mixture to a boil; reduce heat. Cover and simmer for 40 minutes. Remove the chicken; set aside.

3 Skim the fat from the broth; discard. Transfer the broth to a large saucepan; keep hot. Clean the Dutch oven.

4 When the chicken is cool enough to handle, remove the chicken meat from the bones. Discard the skin (if it is still on the chicken) and bones. Chop the chicken meat into bite-size pieces; set aside.

5 To make the roux: In the Dutch oven, stir together the cooking oil and flour until smooth. Cook over medium-high heat for 5 minutes, stirring constantly; reduce heat to medium. Cook and stir about 15 minutes more or until the roux is a dark reddish brown.

6 Stir the celery, onion and green sweet pepper into the roux. Cook over medium heat for 3 to 5 minutes or just until the vegetables are tender, stirring often.

7 Gradually stir in *3 cups* of the reserved chicken broth; refrigerate the remaining chicken broth for another use. Add the okra, *undrained* tomatoes, garlic and hot pepper sauce. Bring the mixture to a boil; reduce heat. Cover and simmer for 20 minutes.

8 Add the chicken to the tomato mixture; heat through. Serve with the hot cooked rice. If desired, garnish with the parsley or green onion tops.

 TIPS FROM OUR KITCHEN

Roux is a French term for a mixture of flour and fat that is cooked and used to thicken sauces and gravies. It is the slow cooking that produces the brown roux used to flavor, thicken and color gumbos. When properly browned, the roux will have a nutty aroma and a dark, reddish brown color similar to that of a tarnished penny.

Nutrition Analysis (*Per Serving*): Calories: 469 / Cholesterol: 66 mg / Carbohydrates: 46 g / Protein: 27 g / Sodium: 708 mg / Fat: 20 g (Saturated Fat: 4 g) / Potassium: 1013 mg.

BUCK'S EASTERN CAROLINA BRUNSWICK STEW

Makes 6 to 8 Servings

1 4- to 5-pound chicken
3 pounds potatoes, peeled and cubed
4 16-ounce cans tomatoes, cut up
2 16-ounce cans midget-size butter beans *or* lima beans, drained
4 ounces salt pork, cubed
2 ounces smoked pork, cubed
1 red (hot) pepper pod
2 11-ounce cans white shoe peg corn (not yellow), drained

◆ ◆ ◆

Mary Hoffler's recipe for Brunswick Stew comes from her husband's family—in fact, it's been in his family so long, "no one remembers who stirred the first pot!" Mr. Hoffler (known by friends as "Buck") has been cooking this stew for forty or fifty years. He reminds us to be sure the fire isn't too hot, to stir often and to make enough to freeze for later.

Mary Hoffler
Bravo!
The Greensboro Symphony Guild
Greensboro
NORTH CAROLINA

1 In a covered Dutch oven, cook the chicken in 6 cups of *water* until tender (See Tip). Remove from heat. Transfer the chicken to a cutting surface. Cool slightly. Skim the fat from the surface of the stock. Discard the fat and reserve the stock.

2 Debone and cube the chicken.

3 Return the stock to the heat and bring to boiling. Add the cubed chicken, potatoes, tomatoes, butter beans or lima beans, salt pork, smoked pork and red pepper pod. Simmer slowly for 1 to 1½ hours or until the vegetables are tender, stirring occasionally to prevent the vegetables from scorching.

4 Add the white shoe peg corn to the stew. Cover and heat through, stirring occasionally.

 TIPS FROM OUR KITCHEN

The cooking time for the chicken changes depending on whether you're using a stewing hen or a broiler-fryer. A stewing hen will cook in about 2 hours. A broiler-fryer will be done in about 50 minutes.

You can substitute bacon for the salt pork and ham for the smoked pork in this recipe.

To save time and add fiber to the meal, don't peel the potatoes.

You may substitute 4 to 5 cups cooked cubed chicken and four 14-ounce cans chicken broth, and eliminate the first step. Also omit the salt pork if you are using canned broth.

Nutrition Analysis *(Per Serving)*: Calories: 748 / Cholesterol: 112 mg / Carbohydrates: 89 g / Protein: 47 g / Sodium: 1619 mg / Fat: 25 g (Saturated Fat: 8 g) / Potassium: 2142 mg.

BUCK'S EASTERN CAROLINA BRUNSWICK STEW

MULLIGATAWNY SOUP

MULLIGATAWNY SOUP

Makes 6 Servings

- 2 tablespoons butter *or* margarine
- 2 stalks celery, finely chopped (¾ cup)
- ½ cup finely chopped onion (1 medium)
- 1 carrot, finely chopped (½ cup)
- 2 tablespoons all-purpose flour
- 2 teaspoons curry powder
- 4 cups chicken broth
- 1 bay leaf
- ½ cup raisins *or* snipped pitted prunes
- ¼ cup finely chopped apple
- ½ teaspoon shredded lemon peel
- ¼ teaspoon salt
- ¼ teaspoon pepper
- ¼ teaspoon dried thyme, crushed
- ½ cup cooked rice
- ½ cup finely chopped cooked chicken
- ½ cup milk *or* light cream

◆　◆　◆

Bill Dodge's mother gave him this recipe for Mulligatawny Soup. He says, "You can vary the ingredients, especially the dried fruits, without the recipe giving you trouble."

Bill Dodge
Cooking By Male
Greater Pittsburgh Commission
For Women
Pittsburgh
PENNSYLVANIA

1 In a large saucepan, melt the butter or margarine. Add the celery, onion and carrot. Cook until tender but not brown.

2 Stir in the flour and curry powder. Cook about 3 minutes. Add the chicken broth, bay leaf, raisins or pitted prunes, apple, lemon peel, salt, pepper and thyme. Simmer for 15 minutes.

3 Add the rice and chicken. Heat through. Just before serving, stir in the milk or light cream.

 TIPS FROM OUR KITCHEN

If you don't have leftover cooked rice, add 2 tablespoons uncooked rice to the broth with the bay leaf, raisins or prunes, apple, lemon peel, salt, pepper and thyme.

Curry powder is a blend of 16 to 20 ground spices, often including cumin, coriander, red pepper, fenugreek, turmeric, cinnamon, allspice, fennel, ginger and black or white pepper.

Cooking the flour-curry powder mixture in the butter or margarine before adding the chicken broth helps to mellow the flavors of spices.

For the cooked chicken, use your microwave oven to cook one 12-ounce chicken breast. Rinse and pat the chicken breast dry, then place it in a baking dish and cover with waxed paper. Micro-cook at 100% power (high) for 5 to 7 minutes or until the chicken is tender and no longer pink.

You can use a food processor to chop the celery, onion and carrot. First, cut the vegetables into 1-inch chunks and place them in the work bowl with a steel blade. Process with on/off turns until the vegetables are chopped to the desired size.

If you want to make this soup ahead of time, refrigerate or freeze it without the milk or light cream. Then, to serve, heat and stir in the milk or cream.

Nutrition Analysis: (*Per Serving*): Calories: 183 / Cholesterol: 24 mg / Carbohydrates: 23 g / Protein: 9 g / Sodium: 702 mg / Fat: 6 g (Saturated Fat: 3 g) / Potassium: 452 mg.

HERBED CREAM OF CHICKEN NOODLE SOUP

Makes 6 Servings

1½ to 2	pounds meaty chicken pieces *or* 2 whole chicken breasts (1½ pounds), skinned, if desired
2	cloves garlic, minced
1	bay leaf
2	stalks celery
2	medium carrots
1	small onion
1	tablespoon snipped parsley
1	teaspoon dried basil, crushed
½	teaspoon dried tarragon, crushed
½	teaspoon salt
¼	teaspoon pepper
6	ounces kluski noodles (2 cups)
2	cups half-and-half *or* light cream
	Toasted, buttered bread crumbs (optional)
	Fresh basil leaves (optional)

◆   ◆   ◆

Gateways "*contains 296 double-tested recipes, contributed by some of the city's most sophisticated hostesses." The cookbook also contains an entertaining guide with wonderful recipes for a variety of special events.*

Gateways
Auxiliary Twigs…Friends of the
St. Louis Children's Hospital
St. Louis
MISSOURI

1 In a 3-quart saucepan, cover the chicken with 7 cups *water*. Bring the water to a boil; reduce heat. Add the garlic and bay leaf. Simmer the mixture about 25 minutes or until the chicken is tender and no longer pink.

2 Transfer the chicken to a large plate; cool. Strain the broth and skim any visible fat from the surface; discard the garlic and bay leaf. Return the broth to the saucepan.

3 Coarsely chop the celery, carrots and onion; add the vegetables to the broth. Stir in the parsley, basil, tarragon, salt and pepper. Cover and simmer about 20 minutes or until the vegetables are cooked through.

4 Add the kluski noodles to the vegetable mixture and simmer, uncovered, for 10 minutes.

5 Meanwhile, when the chicken is cool enough to handle, remove the meat from the bones; discard the skin and bones. Coarsely chop the chicken meat.

6 Add the chicken meat and half-and-half or light cream to the saucepan. Stir all of the ingredients together. Gently cook the soup until it is heated through; *do not boil*. Season the soup with *salt* and *pepper* to taste. Garnish the soup with toasted, buttered bread crumbs and fresh basil leaves, if desired.

TIPS FROM OUR KITCHEN

Remove the chicken skin before cooking to reduce the amount of fat that needs to be skimmed from the broth. If you want to remove most of the remaining fat from the broth, chill the broth overnight. The fat will solidify in a layer on the top that can be removed easily.

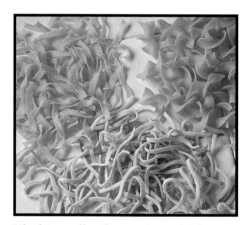

Kluski noodles (bottom) are thicker than ordinary medium (top left) or wide (top right) egg noodles. Frozen or dried egg noodles can be substituted, but they should be cooked separately before adding them to the soup. You should also reduce the water called for in Step 1 to 6 cups.

Nutrition Analysis (*Per Serving*): Calories: 348 / Cholesterol: 106 mg / Carbohydrates: 25 g / Protein: 23 g / Sodium: 310 mg / Fat: 17 g (Saturated Fat: 8 g) / Potassium: 361 mg.

HERBED CREAM OF CHICKEN NOODLE SOUP

GRANDMA THERESA'S TURKEY SOUP

GRANDMA THERESA'S TURKEY SOUP

Makes 8 to 10 Servings

2½ pounds turkey legs, thighs and wings
6   cups water
1   14 ½-ounce can tomatoes with liquid
1   10 ¾-ounce can tomato puree
1¼ cups diced potatoes
½   cup sliced carrots
½   cup chopped celery
½   cup chopped onion
½   teaspoon salt
¼   teaspoon pepper
2   ounces uncooked egg noodles
½   of a 10-ounce package frozen peas, thawed and drained

✦   ✦   ✦

Although Jefferson City, Missouri, is a small town, it houses the headquarters of the state division of the American Cancer Society. This active group proves daily that size has nothing to do with effectiveness. Proceeds from the sale of cookbooks go directly to funding many Cancer Control Programs.

Show Me Missouri
Heritage Cookbook
The American Cancer Society,
Missouri Division
Jefferson City
MISSOURI

1 In a 4-quart Dutch oven, combine the turkey parts with the water; cover and simmer for 2 hours.

2 Transfer the turkey from the Dutch oven to a large bowl and let it cool slightly.

3 When the turkey is cool enough to handle, pull the turkey meat from the bones, cutting it away as needed. Discard the bones and skin. Cut the turkey meat into bite-size pieces; cover and set aside.

4 Using a wide, shallow spoon, skim any fat from the surface of the stock in the Dutch oven. Add the tomatoes with their liquid, tomato puree, potatoes, carrots, celery, onion, salt and pepper to the stock. Cover and simmer the mixture about 30 minutes or until the vegetables are tender. Return the turkey meat to the stock.

5 Stir in the egg noodles and the peas. Cook the soup, uncovered, about 10 minutes or until the peas and noodles are tender.

 TIPS FROM OUR KITCHEN

To make this soup using Thanksgiving leftovers, just skip the directions for simmering the turkey and substitute canned chicken broth (regular or low-sodium) for the water.

If your family prefers chicken, this recipe makes great chicken soup, too. Instead of the turkey, use one broiler-fryer that weighs about 2½ pounds.

Nutrition Analysis *(Per Serving):* Calories: 218 / Cholesterol: 58 mg / Carbohydrates: 19 g / Protein: 25 g / Sodium: 468 mg / Fat: 5 g (Saturated Fat: 1 g) / Potassium: 624 mg.

TURKEY POTPIE

✦ ✦ ✦

According to cookbook chairperson Barbara Hall, 1,000 recipes were received and tastetested for the Thyme & Monet Cookbook. "We had some dinners that were very strange in our house, but we tested every recipe." The committee chose 385 absolutely scrumptious dishes!

Thyme & Monet Cookbook
The Krasl Art Center
St. Joseph
MICHIGAN

1 In a medium saucepan, cover and cook the cubed potatoes in *boiling water* for 20 to 25 minutes or just until tender; set aside. In another medium saucepan, cover and cook the carrots in *boiling water* for 7 to 9 minutes or until tender; set aside.

2 In a large saucepan over medium heat, melt the butter or margarine. Add the mushrooms and onion; cook and stir for 4 to 5 minutes or until the vegetables are tender.

3 Stir in the flour, salt (if using), rosemary and pepper until combined. Stir in the water, whipping cream and bouillon granules. Cook and stir until the mixture is thickened and bubbly. Add the turkey or chicken, sherry, potatoes and carrots and stir to mix all of the ingredients.

4 Preheat the oven to 425°. Spoon the turkey or chicken mixture into a 2-quart casserole dish.

5 Roll out the pastry to fit over the filling. Wrap the pastry around the rolling pin; carefully unroll the pastry over the turkey or chicken mixture. Pinch the pastry around the edges to seal the top and crimp the edge. Cut a

slit in the center of the pastry. Stir together the egg yolk and 1 tablespoon *water*, if desired. Brush the egg-water mixture over the pastry.

6 Bake in the 425° oven for 20 to 25 minutes or until the potpie crust is golden.

 TIPS FROM OUR KITCHEN

You can substitute 2 cups of frozen carrots and peas for the 2 freshly cooked carrots. To thaw the frozen vegetables, place them in a colander and rinse under warm running water.

If you don't have any leftover cooked turkey, bake a 2½- to 3-pound chicken for the necessary 3 cups of cooked meat.

For a fancier top crust: Using miniature cookie or biscuit cutters, work from the center of the pastry out to the edge, repeating cutouts in a pattern and placing them equal distances apart. If the cutouts are too close together, the pastry may rip when it is transferred to the casserole.

Nutrition Analysis (*Per Serving*): Calories: 543 / Cholesterol: 110 mg / Carbohydrates: 38 g / Protein: 28 g / Sodium: 529 mg / Fat: 31 g (Saturated Fat: 31 g) / Potassium: 614 mg.

TURKEY POTPIE

LOUISBURG CHICKEN PIE

LOUISBURG CHICKEN PIE

Makes 8 Servings

- 2 pounds chicken breast *or* turkey breast portion
- 3 medium onions, coarsely chopped
- 3 stalks celery, coarsely chopped
- 6 black peppercorns
- 3 cups water
- 1 pound bulk pork sausage, coarsely crumbled, cooked and drained
- 2 cups cooked, cubed potatoes
- 2 cups sliced fresh mushrooms, cooked and drained
- 1 10-ounce package frozen peas and carrots, thawed
- 1 teaspoon minced garlic
- ½ teaspoon dried rosemary, crushed
- ½ teaspoon dried thyme, crushed
- ½ teaspoon salt
- ¼ teaspoon pepper
- ½ cup all-purpose flour
- ½ cup dry sherry
- Pastry for a 2-crust pie
- 1 egg, beaten

♦   ♦   ♦

From the tiny town of Solebury, Pennsylvania, comes a superb cookbook, which was published to help fund the Trinity Church pre-school.

Dorothy M. Bidelman
<u>Bucks Cooks II</u>
Trinity Church
Solebury
PENNSYLVANIA

1 In a large saucepan or Dutch oven, combine the chicken or turkey with the onions, celery, peppercorns and water. Cover and simmer about 30 minutes or until the poultry is tender. Remove the poultry from the stock. Strain the stock and set aside to cool. (You should have about 3 cups.) Discard the onion, celery and peppercorns.

2 Skin and debone the poultry and cut the meat into bite-size pieces. Set aside.

3 Preheat oven to 375°. Place the chicken or turkey pieces in a 13x9x2-inch baking dish. Add the sausage, potatoes, mushrooms, and peas and carrots.

4 Skim the fat from the cooled stock and place the fat in a medium saucepan. If necessary, add enough margarine or butter to make a total of ¼ cup fat.

5 Melt the fat and stir in the garlic, rosemary, thyme, salt and pepper. Stir in the flour, then add the 3 cups stock and the sherry. Cook, stirring, until thickened and bubbly. Pour the sauce mixture over the poultry and vegetables in the baking dish.

6 On a lightly floured surface, roll out the pastry to extend about 1 inch beyond the edge of the baking dish. Fit the pastry over the dish and flute the edges, pressing the edges firmly on the rim of the dish. Cut several slits in the pastry and brush with the beaten egg.

7 Bake the pie in the 375° oven about 40 minutes or until the crust is golden and the mixture inside the crust is heated through. Let the pie stand 5 minutes before serving.

 TIPS FROM OUR KITCHEN

If you're reluctant to make this main dish pie from scratch, here's a quicker version. Skip simmering the poultry (step 1) and start with 3 cups of cooked chicken or turkey meat and 3 cups canned chicken broth. (You can usually get cooked chicken at supermarket deli counters.) Then, instead of making your own pastry, use refrigerated pie crust.

For a fluted edge, press with your thumb from the inside of the pie against your thumb and forefinger of your other hand.

Nutrition Analysis *(Per Serving)*: Calories: 685 / Cholesterol: 110 mg / Carbohydrates: 47 g / Protein: 34 g / Sodium: 906 mg / Fat: 38 g (Saturated Fat: 11 g) / Potassium: 791 mg.

CHICKEN "POTPIE" WITH CORN BREAD

Makes 6 Servings
Filling:
¼ cup margarine *or* butter
1 cup chopped onion
1 cup sliced celery
1½ cups sliced fresh mushrooms
¼ cup all-purpose flour
1 14½-ounce can chicken broth
1 cup milk
1 10-ounce package frozen peas
½ teaspoon salt
¼ teaspoon dried thyme, crushed
¼ teaspoon pepper
1 cup sliced carrots
3 cups chopped cooked chicken
Biscuits:
½ cup cornmeal
½ cup all-purpose flour
1½ teaspoons sugar
1½ teaspoons baking powder
⅛ teaspoon salt
2 tablespoons margarine *or* butter
1 beaten egg
⅓ cup milk
1 tablespoon snipped parsley

♦ ♦ ♦

According to Norma Baker,
Chicken Potpie with Corn Bread
is an excellent recipe for fall
"when you need to use the oven."
It is a family favorite that Norma
has made for many years.

Norma Baker
Campbell Charity Cookbook
Employees of Campbell Soup Co.
Fayetteville
ARKANSAS

1 Preheat the oven to 425°.

2 To make the filling: In a large sauce-pan over medium-high heat, melt the ¼ cup margarine or butter. Add the onion and celery. Cook and stir for 2 minutes.

3 Add the mushrooms to the sauce-pan; cook and stir about 3 minutes more or until the vegetables are tender. Stir in the ¼ cup flour and cook for 1 minute more.

4 Carefully add the chicken broth and the 1 cup milk; cook and stir over medium heat until thickened and bubbly. Add the peas, the ½ teaspoon salt, the thyme and pepper; set aside.

5 Cook the carrots in 1 cup *boiling water* for 5 minutes; drain. Add the cooked carrots and chicken to the sauce. Spoon the sauce into a 2-quart rectangular baking dish; set aside.

6 To make the biscuits: In a small bowl, stir together the cornmeal, the ½ cup flour, the sugar, baking powder and the ⅛ teaspoon salt. Using a pastry blender or 2 knives, cut in the 2 table-spoons margarine or butter until the mixture resembles coarse crumbs.

7 In another small bowl, stir together the beaten egg, the ⅓ cup milk and the parsley. Add the milk mixture to the crumb mixture; stir until moistened.

8 Evenly spoon mounds of the biscuit mixture over the chicken mixture. Bake in the 425° oven for 20 to 25 minutes or until the filling is bubbly and the biscuits are golden.

 TIPS FROM OUR KITCHEN

You can use leftover cooked turkey in this recipe. Or, start with 2¼ pounds whole chicken breasts (about 2½ medium breasts). Cook the chicken breasts in a large skillet with 2 cups water. Heat to a boil; reduce heat. Cover and simmer the chicken for 20 to 25 minutes or until tender and no longer pink. Drain and cut into cubes.

Cornmeal is made by grinding dried corn kernels. It can be white, yellow or blue depending on the strain. It is best to use yellow cornmeal in this recipe. Store cornmeal in an airtight container in a cool, dry place up to 6 months or in the refrigerator up to 1 year.

Nutrition Analysis (*Per Serving*): Calories: 458 / Cholesterol: 107 mg / Carbohydrates: 37 g / Protein: 32 g / Sodium: 745 mg / Fat: 20 g (Saturated Fat: 5 g) / Potassium: 651 mg.

CHICKEN "POTPIE" WITH CORN BREAD

KATIE'S CHICKEN CASSEROLE

KATIE'S CHICKEN CASSEROLE

Makes 10 Servings

- 1 6-ounce package long grain and wild rice mix
- 3 cups chopped cooked chicken (1 pound)
- 1 tablespoon lemon juice
- 2 10¾-ounce cans condensed cream of celery soup
- 1¼ cups mayonnaise *or* salad dressing
- 1 16-ounce can French-style green beans, drained, *or* one 14-ounce can artichoke hearts, drained and sliced
- 1 8-ounce can sliced water chestnuts, drained
- 1 4-ounce jar sliced pimiento, drained
- 2 cups herb-seasoned stuffing mix
- ¼ cup margarine *or* butter, melted
- ⅓ cup slivered almonds

Sliced pimiento (optional)

♦   ♦   ♦

Katie Frazer has changed this recipe a bit to suit her own taste—she prefers the artichoke hearts to green beans. Since she submitted Katie's Chicken Casserole to Family Secrets, several people have called to tell her how much they enjoy it.

Katie Frazer
Mrs. Stan Hayes
Family Secrets . . .the Best of Delta
Lee Academy
Clarksdale
MISSISSIPPI

1 Preheat the oven to 350°.

2 Prepare the long grain and wild rice mix according to the package directions; set aside.

3 Meanwhile, in a large bowl, stir together the chicken and lemon juice. Stir in the undiluted cream of celery soup, mayonnaise or salad dressing, green beans or artichoke hearts, water chestnuts and pimiento. Stir the cooked rice into the chicken mixture.

4 Spread the chicken-rice mixture into a 3-quart rectangular baking dish. In a medium bowl, stir together the stuffing mix and melted margarine or butter. Sprinkle the stuffing mixture evenly over the chicken-rice mixture.

5 Bake, uncovered, in the 350° oven for 35 minutes. Sprinkle the slivered almonds evenly over the top of the casserole and bake about 10 minutes more or until heated through. Garnish with the sliced pimiento, if desired.

 TIPS FROM OUR KITCHEN

If frozen, chopped cooked chicken isn't available, bake or roast one 2½- to 3-pound chicken. Let the chicken cool slightly and remove the meat from the bones. Package the chicken meat in 3-cup portions; label, date and freeze the cooked chicken.

To make this casserole ahead: Prepare the casserole through Step 3. Cover the baking dish and refrigerate up to 24 hours. To heat for serving: Bake, covered, in a 350° oven for 45 minutes. Sprinkle the slivered almonds evenly over the top of the casserole and bake, uncovered, for 10 to 15 minutes more or until the casserole is heated through.

When packing prepared food for a pot-luck, remember these two rules: Keep hot foods hot and discard any perishable foods that have been sitting at room temperature for 2 hours or more. Use an insulated bag or several layers of newspapers to keep the casserole hot en route. If you have leftovers that were chilled promptly, be sure to reheat them to an internal temperature of 165°.

Nutrition Analysis (*Per Serving*): Calories: 518 / Cholesterol: 63 mg / Carbohydrates: 31 g / Protein: 19 g / Sodium: 1309 mg / Fat: 36 g (Saturated Fat: 6 g) / Potassium: 313 mg.

EASY TURKEY CASSEROLE

Makes 6 Servings
1 6- or 6¼-ounce package regular rice mix *or* curry-flavored rice mix (3 cups prepared)
2 cups cubed cooked turkey
1 10-ounce package frozen green peas
1 10¾-ounce can condensed cream of chicken soup
⅔ cup milk
Paprika (optional)

❖ ❖ ❖

The P.E.O. Sisterhood is a philanthropic and educational organization for women. It is dedicated to many worthy causes, including Topeka Rescue Mission (for the destitute and homeless) and Continuing Education (often for single parents). Every few years, the organization holds a state-wide convention. To defray the costs of the Topeka convention, <u>Recipes Old and New</u> was created; to date approximately 10,000 copies have been sold.

Helen Peterson
<u>Recipes Old and New</u>
Chapter CS of P.E.O.
Topeka
KANSAS

1 Grease a 2-quart casserole dish; set aside.

2 In a large saucepan, prepare the regular or curry-flavored rice mix according to the package directions.

3 Add the cubed turkey, frozen peas (separating the peas), undiluted cream of chicken soup and milk to the rice. Stir until all of the ingredients are well mixed. Turn the turkey mixture into the prepared casserole dish. If desired, generously sprinkle with the paprika.

4 Cover and bake in a 375° oven for 35 to 40 minutes or until the casserole is heated through.

 TIPS FROM OUR KITCHEN

You need 10 to 12 ounces of leftover turkey to equal 2 cups of cubed turkey.

You can easily adapt this basic recipe to suit any taste or mood by trying some of these variations. Substitute cooked chicken or ham for the turkey. Try other flavored rice mixes. Use a different flavor of soup, such as low-sodium cream of mushroom or cream of celery soup. Substitute frozen chopped broccoli or a frozen peas-and-carrots combination for the frozen peas.

If you're concerned about the amount of fat in your diet, use skim milk or substitute ⅓ cup nonfat *dry milk powder* and ½ cup *water*. Be sure to add only the turkey meat, not the skin.

You don't need to preheat the oven because oven temperature is less critical for this type of casserole than it is for a cake.

Nutrition Analysis (*Per Serving*): Calories: 273 / Cholesterol: 51 mg / Carbohydrates: 34 g / Protein: 18 g / Sodium: 1422 mg / Fat: 7 g (Saturated Fat: 2 g) / Potassium: 328 mg.

EASY TURKEY CASSEROLE

CHICKEN, RICE AND BROCCOLI CASSEROLE

CHICKEN, RICE AND BROCCOLI CASSEROLE

Makes 10 Servings

- 1 3½-pound broiler-fryer chicken, cooked *or* 3 cups cubed, cooked chicken *or* turkey
- 1¼ cups beef broth
- 1 cup long grain rice
- ¼ cup butter *or* margarine, cut up
- 1 10½-ounce can condensed French onion soup
- 1 4½-ounce jar sliced mushrooms, drained
- ¼ teaspoon garlic powder
- 2 10-ounce boxes frozen chopped broccoli *or* broccoli spears, thawed and drained
- 1 10¾-ounce can condensed cream of mushroom soup
- ⅔ cup milk
- ¼ cup mayonnaise *or* salad dressing
- ¼ teaspoon Worcestershire sauce
- 1 cup shredded cheddar cheese (4 ounces)

♦   ♦   ♦

Nell Abels told us that this casserole is loved by friends and family. In fact, her son "could eat the whole casserole himself." Nell enjoys preparing the dish, especially because "it smells so good baking!"

Nell Abels
Bravo
The Greensboro Symphony Guild
Greensboro
NORTH CAROLINA

1 Preheat the oven to 325°.

2 If using a roasting chicken, remove the meat from the bones and cut the meat into cubes; set aside.

3 Meanwhile, in a 3-quart rectangular baking dish, stir together the beef broth, uncooked rice, butter or margarine, undiluted French onion soup, mushrooms and garlic powder. Cover the baking dish tightly with aluminum foil. Bake in the 325° oven about 1 hour or until the rice is tender and the liquid has been absorbed. Remove from the oven. Increase the oven temperature to 375°.

4 Stir the rice mixture. Top with the drained broccoli and chicken or turkey.

5 In a medium bowl, stir together the undiluted cream of mushroom soup, milk, mayonnaise or salad dressing and Worcestershire sauce. Spoon the mixture evenly over the chicken or turkey. Sprinkle with the cheddar cheese. Bake the casserole, covered, in the 375° oven for 30 minutes. Uncover and bake about 10 minutes more or until heated through.

 TIPS FROM OUR KITCHEN

Homemade or purchased chicken broth can be used for the beef broth.

For a less salty flavor, use reduced-sodium condensed French onion soup and condensed cream of mushroom soup. Also use reduced-sodium cheddar cheese.

If you are taking this dish to a potluck or picnic, time the cooking so that the casserole is done just before it's time to leave. Then cover the pan with aluminum foil and wrap in several layers of newspaper, or place the pan in an insulated carrier to keep the dish hot. Afterwards, try to chill any leftovers within 2 hours because food safety experts recommend discarding cooked meat or poultry that sits at room temperature for 2 hours or longer. If you have questions about the safety of leftovers, call the U.S. Department of Agriculture's Meat and Poultry Hotline at 1-800-535-4555.

Nutrition Analysis (*Per Serving*): Calories: 419 / Cholesterol: 84 mg / Carbohydrates: 23 g / Protein: 25 g / Sodium: 857 mg / Fat: 25 g (Saturated Fat: 9 g) / Potassium: 371 mg.

DELUXE CHICKEN À LA KING

2 tablespoons butter *or* margarine
1 cup sliced fresh mushrooms
¼ cup chopped green sweet pepper
1 tablespoon chopped onion
2 tablespoons all-purpose flour
¾ teaspoon salt
2 cups half-and-half *or* light cream
2 cups cubed cooked chicken *or* turkey
2 tablespoons dry sherry
1 tablespoon lemon juice
3 egg yolks
¼ cup butter *or* margarine, softened
½ teaspoon paprika
2 tablespoons chopped pimiento

♦   ♦   ♦

In the introduction to Brunch Basket, *the Junior League of Rockford provides a brief history of the many uses of baskets. The connection between baskets and brunch is mentioned throughout the cookbook, with hints on using baskets "to add pizzazz to your family meals and inspire your entertaining."*

Brunch Basket
The Junior League of Rockford
Rockford
ILLINOIS

1 In a large saucepan, melt the 2 tablespoons butter or margarine. Cook the mushrooms, green sweet pepper and onion in the hot butter or margarine until the vegetables are tender. Stir in the flour and salt.

2 Carefully add the half-and-half or light cream all at once. Cook and stir over medium heat until the mixture is thickened and bubbly. Cook and stir for 1 minute more.

3 Add the chicken or turkey, sherry and lemon juice. Continue to cook until the mixture is heated through.

4 Meanwhile, in a small bowl, thoroughly blend the egg yolks, the ¼ cup softened butter or margarine and the paprika; set aside.

5 Bring the chicken mixture to a boil; add the yolk mixture all at once, stirring until well blended. Cook and stir for 1 to 2 minutes more or until the sauce has thickened. Remove from heat; stir in the pimiento.

 TIPS FROM OUR KITCHEN

Serve the Deluxe Chicken à la King on waffles, pastry shells, biscuits, corn bread, toasted English muffins or toast points.

For 2 cups cubed, cooked chicken, start with 2 whole medium chicken breasts (about 1½ pounds), halved and skinned, or ¾ pound of skinned and boned chicken breasts. Place the chicken in a large skillet with 1⅓ cups *water*. Bring to a boil; reduce heat. Cover and simmer for 18 to 20 minutes for breast halves with bones (12 to 14 minutes for boneless pieces) or until the chicken is tender and no longer pink. Drain and cut into cubes.

If you prefer, substitute milk for the sherry.

Nutrition Analysis (*Per Serving*): Calories: 531 / Cholesterol: 318 mg / Carbohydrates: 11 g / Protein: 29 g / Sodium: 698 mg / Fat: 41 g (Saturated Fat: 22 g) / Potassium: 467 mg.

DELUXE CHICKEN Á LA KING

chapter three

meatless
dishes

Increasing numbers of people

are making meatless eating a way of life. Others, in an attempt to broaden their family's diet and to boost their nutritional needs, are including more meals without meat every week. Whatever the motivation, these marvelous meatless recipes will provide enticing eating for all. Who can resist such dining delights as Aunt Ella's Macaroni and Cheese, Pasta with Creamy Basil Sauce, or Eggplant Parmigiana? Hernandez Black Beans is a spicy sensation you serve over rice, and Spinach and Rice Torta gives new meaning to the word "pie." All delicious dishes!

AUNT ELLA'S MACARONI AND CHEESE

AUNT ELLA'S MACARONI AND CHEESE

Makes 4 to 6 Servings

8   ounces elbow macaroni *or* assorted pasta, such as small shells, spirals and wagon wheels (2 cups)

1   tablespoon butter *or* margarine, softened

1   egg, well beaten

1   teaspoon dry mustard

½   teaspoon salt

⅛   teaspoon ground nutmeg

1   tablespoon boiling water

1   cup milk

3   cups shredded sharp cheddar cheese (12 ounces)

¼   cup grated onion

Paprika

♦   ♦   ♦

"If it was Ella's, you knew it would be good." Who is Aunt Ella? If you lived in Wisconsin, you'd surely know—she's quite a famous lady there. In her day, Ella was a caterer in demand, an "effervescent organizer" whose peppy personality and popular menu caught on like wildfire. So, Aunt Ella opened Ella's Deli. Successful? "Everybody knows Ella's," says one of her many local admirers, "because everything she cooked was excellent!"

Sue Marcus
The Best of Beth Israel
Milwaukee
WISCONSIN

1 Preheat oven to 350°. Lightly grease a 1½-quart casserole dish.

2 Cook the macaroni or pasta in boiling water following the package directions until al dente (tender but firm to the bite). Drain the macaroni or pasta, then return it to the saucepan. Stir in the butter and egg.

3 In a large bowl, combine the mustard, salt and nutmeg with the tablespoon of boiling water. Stir in the milk, *2½ cups* of the cheese, the onion and macaroni or pasta.

4 Pour the macaroni mixture into the prepared casserole dish. Top with the remaining cheese. Sprinkle with the paprika.

5 Bake the casserole in the 350° oven for 1 hour or until a well-browned top crust has formed.

TIPS FROM OUR KITCHEN

If you'd like to lower the fat content a bit, substitute skim milk and low-fat cheddar or low-fat American cheese for the whole milk varieties. To lower the sodium content somewhat, use reduced-sodium cheeses and omit the ½ teaspoon of salt.

For an extra-crispy casserole, we baked this in a flat 1½-quart baking dish.

Fresh tomato wedges and a sprig of fresh thyme make a colorful garnish when set against the golden color of the casserole.

Nutrition Analysis *(Per Serving):* Calories: 651 / Cholesterol: 155 mg / Carbohydrates: 49 g / Protein: 32 g / Sodium: 871 mg / Fat: 36 g (Saturated Fat: 21 g) / Potassium: 266 mg.

SPAGHETTI MARCO POLO

Makes 6 Servings

2 tablespoons cooking oil, margarine *or* butter
1 clove garlic, minced
8 ounces spaghetti, cooked and drained
⅔ cup chopped walnuts
½ cup chopped black olives
1 4-ounce jar pimientos, drained and chopped *or* ½ cup chopped roasted sweet red peppers
⅓ cup snipped parsley
1 tablespoon snipped fresh basil *or* ½ teaspoon dried basil, crushed
¼ teaspoon salt
⅛ teaspoon pepper

◆   ◆   ◆

The Sterling Forest Volunteer Fire Company Women's Auxiliary holds fund-raisers to help support the Fire Company, which is only partially supported by taxes. The Auxiliary also provides food and beverages "for the volunteer firemen who have been out in the snow or rain for hours, unable to leave a fire scene." The sale of The Beginning and End *helps to support these efforts.*

Ladies Auxiliary
The Beginning and End
Sterling Forest Volunteer Fire Co.
Tuxedo Park
NEW YORK

1 In a small skillet, heat the oil, margarine or butter. Add the garlic and cook and stir over medium heat until the garlic is golden.

2 Return the drained spaghetti to the saucepan in which it was cooked. Pour the oil mixture over the hot spaghetti. Add the walnuts, olives, pimientos or roasted sweet red peppers, parsley, basil, salt and pepper. Toss the pasta gently to coat all of the strands with the oil mixture. Transfer to a serving dish or platter. Serve hot.

TIPS FROM OUR KITCHEN

To measure 8 ounces of uncooked spaghetti, hold enough 10-inch-long spaghetti in a bunch to measure about 2 inches in diameter. After cooking, this amount will yield about 4 cups.

The entire garlic bulb is sometimes called a head. Each section of the bulb is a clove. When shopping, look for firm, plump garlic bulbs. Store them in a cool, dry, dark place. Leave the bulbs whole until ready to use because the individual cloves dry out quickly. Peeled garlic should be used immediately.

To peel garlic easily, break off a clove from the garlic bulb and place it on a cutting surface. Hold the flat side of a large knife on the clove and hit the knife firmly with the heel of your hand. The peel should pull away easily.

Unshelled walnuts will keep indefinitely in a cool, dry place. Store shelled nuts in an airtight container in the refrigerator and they'll stay fresh for six months. For long-term storage, freeze shelled walnuts up to one year.

Black olives have a smooth, mellow taste. They're sold in cans and come pitted or unpitted, whole, sliced or chopped. For a more distinctive olive flavor in this recipe, you can substitute Italian-style olives. These are usually salt-cured and oil-coated, and can be found in supermarkets, delicatessens and specialty food stores.

For a change in flavor, substitute oregano or thyme for the basil in the recipe.

Nutrition Analysis (*Per Serving*): Calories: 291 / Cholesterol: 0 mg / Carbohydrates: 33 g / Protein: 7 g / Sodium: 147 mg / Fat: 15 g (Saturated Fat: 2 g) / Potassium: 150 mg.

SPAGHETTI MARCO POLO

PASTA WITH CREAMY TOMATO SAUCE

PASTA WITH CREAMY TOMATO SAUCE

Makes 4 to 6 Servings

3	tablespoons olive oil
1½	pounds ripe plum *or* regular tomatoes, coarsely chopped (3½ cups)
1	small onion, chopped (⅓ cup)
1	stalk celery, finely chopped (½ cup)
¼	cup snipped fresh parsley
2	tablespoons snipped fresh basil *or* 2 teaspoons dried basil, crushed
1	teaspoon sugar
½	cup whipping cream
¼	cup olive oil
¼	pound snow peas, halved
1	medium zucchini, chopped (1¼ cups)
2	ripe plum tomatoes, seeded and coarsely chopped
¼	cup thinly sliced green onion
8	ounces angel hair pasta

Grated Parmesan cheese (optional)

◆　◆　◆

Debbie Schall's favorite activity is cooking. For this recipe, Debbie said that she often varies the vegetables depending upon what is available in her garden.

Debbie Schall
<u>*Merrymeeting Merry Eating*</u>
Regional Memorial
Hospital Auxiliary
Brunswick
MAINE

1 In a large saucepan, heat the 3 tablespoons olive oil. Add the 1½ pounds tomatoes, onion, celery, parsley, basil, sugar, ½ teaspoon *salt* and ¼ teaspoon *pepper.* Over medium-high heat, bring the tomato mixture to a boil. Reduce heat and simmer, uncovered, for 30 minutes, stirring occasionally. Remove the saucepan from the heat and let the tomato mixture cool slightly.

2 In an blender container or food processor bowl, blend or process the tomato mixture until pureed. Strain the puree; remove and discard the tomato skins and seeds. Return the tomato mixture to the saucepan. Stir in the whipping cream. Gently heat the tomato sauce through; *do not boil.*

3 Meanwhile, in a large skillet over medium heat, heat the ¼ cup olive oil. Add the snow peas, zucchini, the 2 plum tomatoes, the green onion and ½ teaspoon *salt.* Cook and stir for 4 to 5 minutes or until the vegetables are crisp-tender; set aside.

4 Cook the angel hair pasta according to the package directions; drain. Place the pasta in a serving bowl or on a platter. Add the vegetable mixture; toss. Spoon the tomato sauce over the pasta and sprinkle with Parmesan cheese, if desired

 TIPS FROM OUR KITCHEN

You can cook and puree the tomato sauce (without the cream) the morning or day before serving. Slowly heat the sauce while the vegetables and pasta are cooking. Then stir in the cream just before serving.

Angel hair pasta (right) is spaghetti made into very fine strands. It cooks quickly and absorbs sauces very well. If desired, spaghetti (left), vermicelli or linguine, which are thicker, can be substituted for the angel hair pasta in this recipe.

For a heartier main dish, stir-fry 12-ounces of skinless, boneless chicken breasts that have been cut into strips until the chicken is tender and no longer pink. Add the chicken to the pasta along with the vegetables.

Nutrition Analysis (*Per Serving*): Calories: 640 / Cholesterol: 46 mg / Carbohydrates: 63 g / Protein: 14 g / Sodium: 702 mg / Fat: 38 g (Saturated Fat: 12 g) / Potassium: 785 mg.

PASTA AND ZUCCHINI

Makes 6 Servings

 2   quarts water
 8   ounces large pasta shells
 3   tablespoons margarine *or* butter
2½   cups sliced zucchini
 ¼   cup sliced green onions
 2   cloves garlic, minced
 1   tablespoon snipped parsley
 ½   teaspoon Italian seasoning
 ¼   cup grated Parmesan cheese

✦   ✦   ✦

The Holiday Project is a national organization made up of dedicated volunteers who visit and bring cheer to those who are less fortunate or who are alone. Jeannie Komsky, former chairperson for the San Fernando Valley Committee, tells us that proceeds from cookbook sales go toward purchasing gifts, though she emphasized that it is not the gifts that are important, but the love and caring that accompany each visit.

Marian Hillman
The Holiday Project Cookbook
The Holiday Project
Encino
CALIFORNIA

1 In large kettle, bring the water to a boil. Gradually add the pasta and reduce the heat slightly. Boil for 12 to 15 minutes or until the pasta is tender but firm (al dente).

2 Meanwhile, in a large skillet, melt the margarine or butter. Add the zucchini, green onion, garlic and parsley. Cook and stir about 10 minutes or until the vegetables are tender. Remove from heat. Drain well.

3 Add the pasta to the zucchini mixture along with the Italian seasoning. Heat and toss for 2 to 3 minutes or until heated through and well mixed. Remove from heat. Add *half* of the Parmesan cheese and toss. Sprinkle the remaining Parmesan cheese on top and serve.

TIPS FROM OUR KITCHEN

Al dente (*to the tooth*) is the Italian way of describing pasta that is cooked until tender but still slightly firm.

An easy way to grate Parmesan cheese is to use a food processor. Place the steel blade in the work bowl. Add pieces of Parmesan cheese and process until finely grated. Two ounces of Parmesan cheese will yield ½ cup grated.

For variety, you can change the shapes and colors of the pasta. For instance, try substituting mostaccioli or rigatoni for the shell macaroni.

For another change, substitute yellow summer squash for the zucchini in this recipe.

Nutrition Analysis (*Per Serving*): Calories: 239 / Cholesterol: 3 mg / Carbohydrates: 33 g / Protein: 7 g / Sodium: 159 mg / Fat: 9 g (Saturated Fat: 2 g) Potassium: 131 mg.

PASTA AND ZUCCHINI

PASTA WITH CREAMY BASIL SAUCE

PASTA WITH CREAMY BASIL SAUCE

Makes 4 Servings

6	ounces radiatore *or* rigatoni
1	clove garlic, peeled
1¼	cups lightly packed fresh basil leaves
¾	cup low-fat cottage cheese
¼	teaspoon salt
⅛	teaspoon fresh ground pepper
1	medium tomato, chopped
1	ounce crumbled Gorgonzola *or* blue cheese (optional)
2	tablespoons pine nuts (optional)

❖   ❖   ❖

Diane Fortier combined two recipes to create this wonderful pasta dish. While her children prefer their pasta with a simple spaghetti sauce, she and her husband, Jacques, like the little extra zip that comes from the Gorgonzola cheese. Diane suggests serving this dish with a salad and garlic bread.

Diane Fortier
Wigh Cook?
**St. Gregory the Great Home &
School Association
Danbury
CONNECTICUT**

1 Bring 3 quarts *water* to a boil. Cook the radiatore or rigatoni according to the package directions.

2 Meanwhile, place the garlic in a food processor bowl; process until chopped. Add the basil and cottage cheese; process until smooth. Remove the cover and stir in the salt and pepper.

3 Drain the pasta. Return the pasta to the hot pan. Stir in the basil-cottage cheese sauce. Transfer to a warm serving dish and top with the chopped tomato. Sprinkle with the crumbled Gorganzola and pine nuts, if desired. Serve immediately.

 TIPS FROM OUR KITCHEN

Cooking pasta to the *al dente* stage requires frequent testing near the end of cooking time. The pasta should be tender but still slightly firm when it is bitten.

This sauce works best when prepared in a food processor. The use of a blender is not recommended.

While this sauce can be used on any pasta shape you choose, we found it clings especially well to ruffled or corkscrew pasta.

If fresh basil is not available, you can achieve a similar flavor by using 1¼ cups snipped fresh parsley or spinach plus 1 teaspoon dried basil, crushed.

Nutrition Analysis (*Per Serving*): Calories: 212 / Cholesterol: 4 mg / Carbohydrates: 37 g / Protein: 12 g / Sodium: 310 mg / Fat: 2 g (Saturated Fat: 1 g) / Potassium: 221 mg.

LASAGNA ROLL-UPS

Makes 6 to 8 Servings

12	lasagna noodles

Sauce:

1	tablespoon cooking oil
1	large onion, chopped
1	clove garlic, minced
2	16-ounce cans whole Italian-style (plum) tomatoes, cut up
1	6-ounce can tomato paste
⅔	cup water
3	tablespoons snipped parsley
1	tablespoon sugar
1	teaspoon salt
1	teaspoon dried oregano, crushed
¼	teaspoon pepper
2	15-ounce containers ricotta cheese
2	cups shredded mozzarella cheese (8 ounces)
½	cup grated Parmesan cheese
2	eggs, well beaten

♦ ♦ ♦

__There's More to Lima than Beans__ is a wonderful cookbook compiled by the Lima and Allen County Medical Alliance to raise funds "to maintain current and future health education projects."

Charlotte Ditter
__There's More to Lima than Beans__
The Lima and Allen County
Medical Alliance
Lima
OHIO

1 In a large saucepan, cook the lasagna noodles in boiling, *salted water* for 10 to 12 minutes or until tender; drain. Rinse with cool water and drain again. Set aside.

2 To make the sauce: In a large skillet, heat the oil. Add the onion and garlic and cook until tender. Carefully add the *undrained* tomatoes, tomato paste, water, *2 tablespoons* of the parsley, the sugar, salt, oregano and pepper. Simmer, uncovered, for 20 minutes.

3 Meanwhile, in a large mixing bowl, stir together the ricotta cheese, *1 cup* of the mozzarella cheese, the Parmesan cheese, eggs and the remaining parsley. Preheat the oven to 350°.

4 To assemble: Spread approximately *⅓ cup* of the cheese mixture evenly over *each* of the lasagna noodles.

5 Starting from a short side, roll up each of the lasagna noodles.

6 Pour *half* of the sauce into a 3-quart rectangular baking dish. Place rolled-up noodles seam side down in the baking dish. Top with the remaining sauce.

7 Cover and bake in the 350° oven for 45 minutes. Uncover and sprinkle with the remaining mozzarella cheese. Bake for 5 minutes more. Let stand for 10 to 15 minutes before serving.

___

TIPS FROM OUR KITCHEN

Adding the cheese for the last 5 minutes only prevents it from sticking to the foil during baking.

This casserole adapts well to make-ahead preparation. Refrigerate the covered dish of roll-ups overnight. To serve: Bake in a 350° oven for 1 hour. Uncover and sprinkle with the remaining mozzarella cheese. Bake for 5 minutes more. Let stand for 10 to 15 minutes before serving.

Nutrition Analysis (*Per Serving*): Calories: 602 / Cholesterol: 143 mg / Carbohydrates: 56 g / Protein: 39 g / Sodium: 1179 mg / Fat: 25 g (Saturated Fat: 13 g) / Potassium: 937 mg.

LASAGNA ROLL-UPS

PASTA NESTS AND VEGETABLES

PASTA NESTS AND VEGETABLES

Makes 12 Servings

4 cups fresh cauliflower, broccoli and carrots, cut into small pieces
4 tablespoons butter *or* margarine
3 tablespoons all-purpose flour
1 teaspoon finely shredded lemon peel
½ teaspoon salt
Dash pepper
1½ cups milk
2 8-ounce cartons dairy sour cream
1 12-ounce package dried fettuccine, cooked and drained
2 beaten eggs
½ cup grated Parmesan cheese

◆　◆　◆

Because Sue Miller loves pasta and vegetables, her aunt's recipe for Pasta Nests and Vegetables really appealed to her. Sue also likes the very different presentation of the dish. She usually serves this as a side dish with a basic meat or pork loin, and she sometimes adjusts the recipe, adding onions and other herbs as well as extra cheese.

Sue Miller
Dinner by Design
Everywoman's Resource Center
Topeka
KANSAS

1 Preheat the oven to 350°.

2 Cook the cauliflower, broccoli and carrot pieces in a small amount of *boiling water* for 5 to 10 minutes or until the vegetables are crisp-tender. Drain the vegetable mixture; set aside.

3 In a saucepan, melt the butter or margarine. Stir in the flour, shredded lemon peel, salt and pepper. Add the milk, stirring constantly, until the ingredients are well blended and the mixture is smooth. Cook and stir until the mixture is thickened and bubbly.

4 Stir the sour cream and vegetable mixture into the milk mixture. Bring the mixture *almost* to a boil; remove from heat. Spoon *half* of the vegetable-sauce mixture into a 3-quart rectangular baking dish.

5 Place the cooked fettuccine in a large bowl. Add the beaten eggs and Parmesan cheese; toss until well coated.

6 Using a long-tined fork, twirl several strands of the fettuccine around the tines.

7 Using a second fork, push the twirled pasta strands off into the baking dish, arranging the strands to form a "nest." Repeat with the remaining pasta to make a total of 12 nests.

8 Spoon the remaining vegetable-sauce mixture *around* the pasta nests. Loosely cover the baking dish with aluminum foil. Bake in the 350° oven for 20 to 25 minutes or until heated through.

 TIPS FROM OUR KITCHEN

You can substitute one 16-ounce package of loose-pack frozen broccoli, cauliflower and carrots for the fresh vegetables in this recipe. Cook the frozen vegetables according to the package directions until the vegetables are crisp-tender. Drain the vegetables and cut them into small pieces.

Half of a medium lemon yields about 1 teaspoon of shredded lemon peel.

Nutrition Analysis (*Per Serving*): Calories: 325 / Cholesterol: 79 mg / Carbohydrates: 29 g / Protein: 10 g / Sodium: 301 mg / Fat: 19 g (Saturated Fat: 11 g) / Potassium: 227 mg.

PASTA FLORENTINE

Makes 10 Side-Dish Servings

2 10-ounce packages frozen, chopped spinach
½ cup chopped onion
8 ounces uncooked spaghetti
½ cup grated Parmesan cheese
1 4-ounce jar chopped pimientos, drained
4 tablespoons butter, softened
2 eggs, slightly beaten
3 cups sliced fresh mushrooms
1 14 *or* 15-ounce jar meatless spaghetti sauce
2 cups shredded mozzarella cheese (8-ounces)

◆   ◆   ◆

Adele Adatto, one of the Artist's Palate Cookbook editors, varies her Pasta Florentine recipe to suit her family's moods. While the meatless version featured here is her favorite, she says that she sometimes adds ground beef for a change.

Adele Adatto
Artist's Palate Cookbook
New Orleans Museum of Art
New Orleans
LOUISIANA

1 In a saucepan, place the frozen spinach and the chopped onions. Cook the spinach according to the spinach package directions. Drain well.

2 In a blender or food processor, purée the cooked spinach and onion mixture. Set aside.

3 Preheat oven to 375°.

4 Cook the spaghetti according to the package directions. Drain well.

5 In a large bowl, combine the spinach mixture, cooked spaghetti, Parmesan cheese, pimientos, *2 tablespoons* of the butter and the eggs. Mix well and transfer to a greased 13x9x2-inch baking dish.

6 In a saucepan, cook the mushrooms in the remaining butter for 5 minutes. Add the cooked mushrooms to the spaghetti sauce.

7 Pour the sauce over the spaghetti mixture. Cover and bake in the 375° oven for 25 minutes.

8 Uncover and sprinkle the mozzarella cheese over the top. Bake about 5 minutes longer or until the cheese is melted.

 TIPS FROM OUR KITCHEN

When you're in a hurry, skip the step of puréeing the spinach and simply combine it with the spaghetti, Parmesan cheese, pimientos, butter and eggs.

To turn this recipe into a main dish, add some chopped, cooked beef, pork, chicken or turkey.

Add a garnish of parsley and pimiento to bring just the right amount of color to this dish.

Nutrition Analysis (*Per Serving*): Calories: 292 / Cholesterol: 72 mg / Carbohydrates: 30 g / Protein: 15 g / Sodium: 507 mg / Fat: 13 g (Saturated Fat: 7 g) / Potassium: 481 g.

PASTA FLORENTINE

EGGPLANT PARMIGIANA

EGGPLANT PARMIGIANA

1 Preheat the oven to 350°. Lightly grease a 2-quart rectangular baking dish; set aside.

2 Peel the eggplant and cut crosswise into ¼-inch-thick slices. Place the beaten eggs in a shallow dish; place the bread crumbs in another shallow dish.

3 Dip the eggplant slices, one at a time, into the beaten eggs, then into the bread crumbs, until *each* slice is completely coated.

4 In a large skillet, heat the olive oil. Working in batches if necessary, cook the coated eggplant slices about 4 minutes or until the slices are golden brown on each side, adding additional olive oil as needed. Remove eggplant slices and drain on paper towels.

5 Arrange a single layer of cooked eggplant slices over the bottom of the prepared baking dish. Sprinkle the slices with *one-third* of the grated Parmesan cheese and the oregano. Top with *one-fourth* of the mozzarella cheese slices. Pour *1 can* of the tomato sauce over the layers in the dish. Repeat with 2 more layers, ending with the last can of tomato sauce. Place the remaining slices of mozzarella cheese over the top layer of sauce. Sprinkle with additional Parmesan cheese, if desired.

6 Bake, uncovered, in the 350° oven for 25 to 30 minutes or until heated through.

7 Garnish with sprigs of fresh oregano, if desired.

TIPS FROM OUR KITCHEN

When shopping for eggplant, choose one that is plump, glossy and heavy. The cap should be fresh-looking, tight and free of mold. Keep the eggplant refrigerated and use it within 2 days.

You'll need to start with 6 slices of dried bread to yield 1½ cups of fine dry bread crumbs. Tear the slices and place them in a blender container or food processor bowl. Blend or process until the bread forms fine crumbs. Or, place broken pieces of dried bread in a heavy plastic bag and crush them with a rolling pin.

Nutrition Analysis (*Per Serving*): Calories: 426 / Cholesterol: 101 mg / Carbohydrates: 26 g / Protein: 16 g / Sodium: 926 mg / Fat: 30 g (Saturated Fat: 8 g) / Potassium: 571 mg.

SPINACH AND RICE TORTA

The Morning Star School is located in Pinellas Park, Florida, and annually serves about 60 exceptional children of elementary school age who have a variety of learning problems. Parents and administrators work together to cultivate an "openness, a respect for the individual child and a positive, loving approach to learning that are the keys to the success" of the students at the Morning Star School.

Lydia Dondero
Another Spoonful of Love
Morning Star School
Pinellas Park
FLORIDA

1 Preheat the oven to 350°. Grease the bottom and sides of an 8x8x2-inch baking pan or a 2-quart square baking dish with olive oil. Sprinkle the bread crumbs over the pan; shake the pan to distribute the bread crumbs evenly over the oiled areas; set aside.

2 Squeeze any excess water from the thawed spinach. In a medium bowl, stir together the spinach, rice, the 3 beaten eggs, ricotta or cottage cheese, Parmesan cheese and pepper until all of the ingredients are well mixed.

3 Turn the spinach-rice mixture into the prepared pan or dish. Beat the remaining egg and using a pastry brush, brush the beaten egg over the top of the spinach-rice mixture.

4 Bake in the 350° oven about 45 minutes or until the torta is firm.

 TIPS FROM OUR KITCHEN

To make 3 cups of cooked rice: In a saucepan, bring 2 cups *water* to a boil. Slowly stir in 1 cup *white* or *brown* rice. Return the mixture to a boil; reduce heat. Cover and simmer for 15 minutes for white rice and 35 minutes for brown rice. Remove from heat; let the rice stand, covered, for 5 minutes.

If desired, substitute a wild rice mixture for the cooked rice in this recipe. Prepare the rice according to the package directions.

Ricotta cheese is a fresh moist, white cheese that is very mild and semisweet. It has a soft and slightly grainy texture. Ricotta can be made from whey or from whole or part-skim milk.

Wrap any leftover torta in aluminum foil and refrigerate or freeze it. To reheat: Thaw the torta pieces (if they were frozen). In a buttered skillet over medium heat, cook the torta pieces for 5 minutes, turning once. Or, to microcook: Place 1 serving on a microwave-safe plate; cover and micro-cook on 100% power (high) for 1½ minutes.

Nutrition Analysis (*Per Serving*): Calories: 216 / Cholesterol: 112 mg / Carbohydrates: 20 g / Protein: 13 g / Sodium: 308 mg / Fat: 9 g (Saturated Fat: 4 g) / Potassium: 158 mg.

SPINACH AND RICE TORTA

SPINACH AND PASTA CASSEROLE

SPINACH AND PASTA CASSEROLE

Makes 16 to 20 Side-Dish or 8 Meatless Main-Dish Servings

1½ cups orzo pasta
1 cup chopped onion
2 tablespoons butter *or* margarine
2 10-ounce packages frozen chopped spinach, thawed and well drained
¼ teaspoon salt
¼ teaspoon pepper
3 eggs, beaten
Cream Sauce:
3 cups whole milk
1 medium onion, sliced
1 bay leaf
1 teaspoon whole black peppercorns
¼ teaspoon salt
¼ cup butter *or* margarine
⅓ cup all-purpose flour
2 eggs
Assembly and Topping:
1 cup grated Parmesan cheese
¼ cup butter *or* margarine, melted
1 cup fine dry bread crumbs

♦ ♦ ♦

Profits from the sale of <u>Continental Cuisine Cookbook</u> help to support Nick Triantafillis's philanthropic ventures, particularly his unselfish devotion to aiding the hungry.

Helen Paliouras
<u>Continental Cuisine Cookbook</u>
Nick's Cuisine
Burlington
NORTH CAROLINA

1 Preheat the oven to 350°. Grease a 3-quart rectangular baking dish; set aside. Cook the orzo according to the package directions; drain. Rinse with cold water; drain and set aside.

2 In a medium saucepan, cook the 1 cup chopped onion in the 2 tablespoons butter or margarine until the onion is tender and golden. Add the spinach, the ¼ teaspoon salt and the pepper; remove from heat. Stir in the 3 beaten eggs. Set aside.

3 To make the cream sauce: In a medium saucepan, stir together the milk, the sliced onion, the bay leaf, peppercorns and the ¼ teaspoon salt. Bring to a boil. Remove from heat. In another saucepan, melt the ¼ cup butter or margarine. Stir in the flour until smooth.

4 Strain the milk mixture; add the strained mixture, all at once, to the flour mixture. Cook, stirring constantly, until the sauce is thickened. In a small bowl, beat the 2 eggs. Stir *1 cup* of the sauce into the beaten eggs, then return all of the egg mixture to the saucepan. Cook and stir until the cream sauce is bubbly.

5 To assemble the casserole: Spread *half* of the orzo evenly into the bottom of

the prepared baking dish. Sprinkle ⅓ *cup* of the Parmesan cheese over the orzo. Spoon the spinach mixture over the cheese and cover with the remaining orzo. Sprinkle with another *⅓ cup* of the cheese. Spread the prepared cream sauce over the top.

6 Stir together the ¼ cup melted butter or margarine, the bread crumbs and the remaining cheese; sprinkle over the casserole. Bake, uncovered, in the 350° oven for 40 to 45 minutes or until heated through.

TIPS FROM OUR KITCHEN

Thaw the spinach by placing the packages in a bowl in the refrigerator overnight. Or, unwrap the packages and place the frozen blocks in a strainer. Hold the frozen spinach under warm, running water until it is thawed, using a fork to help break up chunks. Drain the spinach thoroughly to prevent the casserole from becoming watery. If desired, place the thawed spinach in a clean nonterry towel and squeeze gently.

Nutrition Analysis (*Per Serving*): Calories: 257 / Cholesterol: 97 mg / Carbohydrates: 25 g / Protein: 11 g / Sodium: 380 mg / Fat: 13 g (Saturated Fat: 7 g) / Potassium: 256 mg.

HERNANDEZ BLACK BEANS

Makes 4 Servings

- 8 ounces dried black beans (1⅓ cups)
- 1 teaspoon salt
- 1 medium onion, quartered
- ½ sweet green pepper, chopped
- ¼ cup olive oil
- 3 cloves garlic, crushed
- 1 small bay leaf
- ⅛ teaspoon dried oregano, crushed
- 4 cups cooked long-grain rice (optional)

❖ ❖ ❖

Beans and rice are staples in many homes across this country and many countries in Latin America because of their low cost, ease of storage and nutritional value. Dee Couvelha found this recipe as a result of her search for a dish that would duplicate one her mother used to make. She says that it is simple to prepare and consistently delicious.

Dee Couvelha
(with thanks to El Loro Verde Restaurant of Key West, Florida)
A Culinary Celebration
Sheltering Arms Hospitals
Richmond
VIRGINIA

1 Rinse the beans in cool water. In a large bowl, cover beans with 4 cups *water* and soak overnight. For an alternate soaking method: Rinse the beans. In a large saucepan, combine the beans and 4 cups *water*. Bring to boiling; reduce heat. Simmer for 2 minutes. Remove from heat. Cover and let stand for 1 hour.

2 Using the same water, bring the beans to boiling in a large pot. Reduce the heat to medium-low.

3 Add the salt; cover and simmer about 45 minutes or until the beans are tender. Test by pinching a bean. If it is soft and splits, it's done.

4 Add the onion, pepper, olive oil, garlic, bay leaf and oregano to the cooked beans. Cover the pot and simmer about 20 minutes or until the gravy is thick and creamy.

5 If there is too much liquid, remove the lid and cook about 10 minutes more to reduce the liquid. Be careful not to burn. Serve with rice, if desired.

 TIPS FROM OUR KITCHEN

Experts suggest that beans are more easily digestible if you change the water after cooking them. For the best results, drain the beans, rinse them and add 3 cups of fresh water. Then add the rest of the ingredients *except* for the rice.

For more highly seasoned beans, add an extra clove or two of garlic and increase the oregano to ¼ or ½ teaspoon.

Nutrition Analysis (*Per Serving*): Calories: 306 / Cholesterol: 00 mg / Carbohydrates: 34 g / Protein: 12 g / Sodium: 535 mg / Fat: 14 g (Saturated Fat: 2 g)/ Potassium: 527 mg.

HERNANDEZ BLACK BEANS

LENTIL SOUP

LENTIL SOUP

8	cups water *or* chicken broth
3	cups lentils, rinsed (1¼ pounds)
1	teaspoon salt
1	cup chopped onion
1	cup chopped carrot
1	cup chopped celery
1	clove garlic, minced
1½	cups chopped tomatoes
2	tablespoons dry red wine
2	tablespoons lemon juice
1½	tablespoons brown sugar *or* cognac
1	tablespoon wine vinegar
½	teaspoon pepper

♦   ♦   ♦

The Fontbonne Auxiliary provides financial and other assistance to the St. John Hospital and Medical Center and to the Sisters of St. Joseph of Nazareth in Michigan. Through the Auxiliary's efforts, they contribute close to one-half million dollars yearly to the Hospital. Proceeds from the sale of Renaissance Cuisine *help them to achieve this worthwhile feat.*

Janice Hoski
Renaissance Cuisine
The Fontbonne Auxiliary of St. John Hospital
Detroit
MICHIGAN

1 In a 4½-quart Dutch oven, combine the water or chicken broth, lentils and salt. Cover and simmer for 20 minutes.

2 Meanwhile, steam the onion, carrot, celery and garlic over boiling *water* for 8 minutes. Add the steamed vegetables to the lentil mixture.

3 Add the tomatoes, red wine, lemon juice, brown sugar or cognac, wine vinegar and pepper to the Dutch oven. Simmer for 20 minutes. Ladle into soup bowls to serve.

━━━◆━━━

 TIPS FROM OUR KITCHEN

Transform water into chicken broth by adding 2 tablespoons *instant chicken bouillon granules* to 8 cups *water*.

If desired, add spicy smoked sausage or left-over ham to this soup.

You'll need 2 medium tomatoes to equal the 1½ cups chopped tomatoes.

Instead of steaming the vegetables, cook them in 2 tablespoons *butter* or *margarine*, if desired. Or, the uncooked vegetables can be added at the beginning of cooking along with the lentils. Cook as directed for 20 minutes before adding the tomatoes and other flavorings.

Thyme, oregano and/or basil can be added to the soup for additional flavor. Add 1 tablespoon snipped fresh or 1 teaspoon crushed dried herbs with the tomatoes.

Lentils are among the oldest known foods. They contain fewer of the gas-producing sugars than dried beans. To rinse lentils, place them in a strainer and hold under running water.

Nutrition Analysis (*Per Serving*): Calories: 371 / Cholesterol: 0 mg / Carbohydrates: 67 g / Protein: 26 g / Sodium: 572 mg / Fat: 1 g (Saturated Fat: 0 g) / Potassium: 1383 mg.

PARMESAN CORN CHOWDER

Makes 6 to 8 Servings

2 cups chopped peeled potato
½ cup thinly sliced carrot
½ cup thinly sliced celery
¼ cup chopped onion
¼ teaspoon pepper
¼ cup margarine *or* butter
¼ cup all-purpose flour
2 cups milk
1 cup freshly grated Parmesan cheese
1 17-ounce can cream-style corn

◆   ◆   ◆

The All Saints' Episcopal Church began in the 1860s with a small group of individuals gathering for worship in local homes. About thirty years later, they were recognized as the All Saints' Episcopal Church. In 1969, the group merged with a small mission church and erected the present church; since that time, the congregation has grown to four hundred communicants. The Churchmouse Cookbook was created to raise funds for the church's many community projects.

Vera McIntosh
The Churchmouse Cookbook
All Saints' Episcopal Churchwomen
Concord
NORTH CAROLINA

1 In a large Dutch oven, stir together 2 cups *water*, the potato, carrot, celery, onion and pepper. Bring to a boil. Reduce heat; cover and simmer for 10 minutes.

2 Meanwhile, in a large saucepan, melt the margarine or butter. Stir in the flour. Add the milk all at once. Cook and stir over medium heat until the mixture is thickened and bubbly. Cook and stir for 1 minute more.

3 Add the cheese, stirring until it is melted. Carefully add the cheese mixture to vegetable mixture. Stir in the corn. Heat the soup through, stirring occasionally. *Do not boil.*

 TIPS FROM OUR KITCHEN

Freshly grated Parmesan cheese will melt better and give the soup a smoother texture than prepackaged Parmesan. You can use a food processor or grate it by rubbing a piece of cheese over a grater. A hand grater has tiny punched holes and rough, irregular edges, unlike the larger holes or smooth-edged slits of a shredder. For 1 cup of grated cheese, you'll need 4 ounces of ungrated Parmesan cheese.

Chowder usually designates a thick soup made with milk. Do the final heating over a medium to low heat to avoid boiling—and curdling—the milk.

To make preparation even easier and the soup lower in fat, omit the melting margarine step. Instead, combine the milk, flour and cheese; stir into soup.

If desired, sprinkle crisply cooked, crumbled bacon over the top of each serving.

Nutrition Analysis (*Per Serving*): Calories: 316 / Cholesterol: 19 mg / Carbohydrates: 36 g / Protein: 13 g / Sodium: 720 mg / Fat: 15 g (Saturated Fat: 6 g) / Potassium: 492 mg.

PARMESAN CORN CHOWDER

AUNT BEE'S FRENCH ONION SOUP

Makes 10 Servings

- 2 pounds yellow onions, thinly sliced (8 cups)
- 3 tablespoons margarine *or* butter
- 1 tablespoon cooking oil
- 2 tablespoons molasses
- 1 teaspoon sugar
- 3 tablespoons all-purpose flour
- 5 14½-ounce cans beef broth
- ¼ cup vermouth *or* dry white wine
- 10 slices French bread, toasted
- 2 cups shredded Swiss, mozzarella *or* Monterey Jack cheese (8 ounces)

♦   ♦   ♦

Mollie Nichols's recipe for French Onion Soup is a true family favorite. In fact, her husband, Wayne, highly recommends that everyone try it and suggests using a nice Chardonnay rather than the vermouth. Wayne's Aunt Bee, who was a marvelous cook, developed this recipe from scratch and passed it along to Mollie. Mollie tells us that this is a perfect soup to serve for a luncheon.

Mollie Nichols
Great Plains Cooking
P.E.O. Chapter AA
Wray
COLORADO

1 In a 4-quart kettle or Dutch oven, combine the onions, margarine or butter and oil. Cover and cook over medium to low heat for 15 minutes, stirring occasionally.

2 Stir in the molasses and sugar. Cover and simmer for 35 minutes, stirring occasionally.

3 Add the flour; cook and stir for 1 minute.

4 Preheat the oven to 400°. Add the beef broth and vermouth or dry white wine to the onion mixture. Bring to a boil. Cover and simmer for 20 minutes.

5 Ladle the soup into 10 ovenproof bowls and top with the toasted bread. Sprinkle the cheese on top of the bread.

6 Place the bowls (5 at a time) on a 15x10x1-inch baking pan. Bake in the 400° oven about 2 minutes or until the cheese melts.

 TIPS FROM OUR KITCHEN

A food processor makes slicing the onions easier. Cut medium- to large-size onions in half, then carefully wedge them in the feed tube.

If you don't have ovenproof soup bowls, place the toasted bread on a baking sheet. Sprinkle the cheese on the bread and broil 3 inches from the heat for 45 to 60 seconds or until the cheese melts and turns golden. Ladle the soup into bowls and float the cheese-topped bread on top.

Regular beef broth may be too salty for your taste or diet. If so, look for low-sodium broth and use it for all or part of the total amount.

If you prefer to make this recipe without alcohol, omit the vermouth or white wine.

Nutrition Analysis (*Per Serving*): Calories: 376 / Cholesterol: 26 mg / Carbohydrates: 39 g / Protein: 17 g / Sodium: 1,255 mg / Fat: 16 g (Saturated Fat: 7 g) / Potassium: 432 mg.

seafood

The sea has fascinated men and women

for centuries—as a passage to other lands, as a source of adventure, and, closer to home, as the ample provider of diverse and delectable foods. This "catch" of recipes includes exquisite Clam Linguine, bountiful Cioppino, and intriguing Mildred Kemp's Secret Ingredient Crab Soup. Dive into flavorful Florida Fish Chowder or float away on airy Tuna Fish Soufflé. From classic Tuna-Noodle Casserole to creative Leocadia's Seafood Stew, every dish is a pearl beyond price.

CLAM LINGUINE

1	8-ounce package dry linguine
1	6½-ounce can minced clams
2	tablespoons olive oil
2	tablespoons margarine *or* butter
2	cloves garlic, minced
¼ to ½	teaspoon pepper
¼	teaspoon dried basil, crushed
¼	teaspoon dried oregano, crushed
Salt	
2	tablespoons snipped parsley
Grated Parmesan cheese (optional)	

◆　◆　◆

The Stanford University Medical Center Auxiliary was established in 1929 to support the Old Peninsula Hospital in Palo Alto. In 1959, the auxiliary moved to the Stanford University Medical Center and became incorporated as an in-hospital service organization. Their cookbook is one of several fund-raisers hosted by the auxiliary.

Stanford University Medical Center Auxiliary Cookbook
Stanford University Medical Center Auxiliary
Stanford
CALIFORNIA

1 Cook the linguine according to the package directions; drain and keep hot.

2 Meanwhile, drain the clams; reserve the liquid and set aside.

3 In a 2-quart saucepan over medium-high heat, heat the olive oil and margarine or butter until the olive oil is hot and the margarine or butter is melted. Add the garlic; cook and stir for 2 to 3 minutes (do not brown the garlic).

4 Carefully add the reserved clam liquid, pepper, basil, oregano and salt to taste to the saucepan. Reduce heat and simmer, uncovered, for 3 minutes. Stir in the clams; simmer until heated through. Stir the parsley into the clam sauce.

5 Pour the clam sauce over the hot linguine and toss gently to mix the ingredients. Sprinkle with the Parmesan cheese, if desired. Serve immediately.

 TIPS FROM OUR KITCHEN

Clam lovers may want to double the amount of clams. Use the liquid from only 1 can, however.

You can substitute ¼ teaspoon of dried, minced garlic or garlic powder for the garlic cloves in this recipe. Or, try using 1 teaspoon of bottled minced garlic.

Keep the ingredients for this recipe on hand for unexpected guests or for whenever your day doesn't go as planned and you need an easy-to-prepare dinner.

This clam sauce can also be served with other types of pasta, such as spinach noodles, spaghetti or fettuccine.

Nutrition Analysis (*Per Serving*): Calories: 360 / Cholesterol: 29 mg / Carbohydrates: 47 g / Protein: 12 g / Sodium: 127 mg / Fat: 14 g (Saturated Fat: 2 g) / Potassium: 138 mg.

CLAM LINGUINE

LEOCADIA'S SEAFOOD STEW

LEOCADIA'S SEAFOOD STEW

Makes 4 to 6 Servings

1	medium onion, finely chopped
2	tablespoons olive oil
1 to 1½	pounds fresh tuna *or* shark, cut into 1-inch pieces
2	tomatoes, peeled, seeded and finely chopped
¼	cup snipped parsley
2	cloves garlic, minced
2	medium potatoes, chopped
1	bay leaf

Pinch of ground red pepper

4	ounces fresh *or* frozen peas
¼	teaspoon salt
⅛	teaspoon pepper

Toast triangles

♦   ♦   ♦

Leocadia Iribar and her fisher-man husband, Paul, are from Orio, Spain. Paul and his crews often stay out on the ocean for three weeks at a time bringing back mostly tuna, lobster and hake. In this recipe, Leocadia brings out the wonderful flavor of fresh tuna.

Leocadia Iribar
The Art of Basque Cooking
Friends of the Workshop,
Woodland Rehabilitation and
Employment Industries
Woodland
CALIFORNIA

1 In a large skillet, cook the onion in hot oil until tender but not brown. Add *half* of the fish and cook for 2 to 3 minutes, turning the pieces to brown all of the sides. Repeat with the remaining fish.

2 Add the tomatoes, parsley and garlic to the skillet and cook for 2 minutes. Add the potatoes, bay leaf and ground red pepper. Simmer, covered, for 30 minutes, stirring occasionally.

3 Add the peas and cook about 10 minutes more until tender. Remove the bay leaf. Sprinkle with the salt and pepper. Serve with the toast triangles.

TIPS FROM OUR KITCHEN

Cutting the fish into 1-inch pieces will help to cook it more quickly and evenly.

Be sure to use a firm-textured fish in this recipe. If shark or tuna is unavailable, try swordfish.

When selecting fresh peas, choose small, plump, bright green, shiny pods that are filled with medium-size peas. Refrigerate peas in their pods, unwashed, in a plastic bag up to two days. Shell them just before using.

Nutrition Analysis (*Per Serving*): Calories: 377 / Cholesterol: 47 mg / Carbohydrates: 30 g / Protein: 33 g / Sodium: 262 mg / Fat: 14 g (Saturated Fat: 3 g) / Potassium: 843 mg.

Cioppino

Makes 8 Servings

2	tablespoons olive oil
1½	cups chopped onion
1	cup chopped sweet green pepper
3	14½-ounce cans Italian-style plum tomatoes
2	cups dry red wine
¼	cup snipped fresh basil
2	tablespoons tomato paste
1½	teaspoons dried oregano, crushed
1½	teaspoons dried thyme, crushed
¼ to ½	teaspoon dried hot red pepper flakes
1	bay leaf
1	pound fresh *or* frozen halibut *or* scrod, cut into 1½-inch pieces
12	ounces fresh *or* frozen shrimp in shells
12	ounces fresh *or* frozen scallops
24	clams in shell
¼	teaspoon pepper
½	cup finely snipped parsley

◆　　◆　　◆

"This is absolutely the easiest dish to make for company!" recommends Jane Citron, who devised this delicious dish to instruct students in her cooking technique classes.

Jane Citron
The Best of the Best
Rodef Shalom Sisterhood
Pittsburgh
PENNSYLVANIA

1 Pour the oil into a large kettle. Add the onion and sweet green pepper. Cook and stir over low heat until the vegetables are tender.

2 Carefully add the *undrained* tomatoes, red wine, basil, tomato paste, oregano, thyme, pepper flakes and bay leaf. Bring to a boil; reduce heat and simmer, covered, for 1 hour.

3 Meanwhile, thaw the halibut or scrod, shrimp and scallops, if frozen.

4 Shell the shrimp, leaving the tails on. Clean the clams.

5 Uncover the sauce and return to a boil. Stir in the clams. Boil, covered, about 5 minutes or until the clams open. Discard any clams that do not open. Remove all of the clams from the sauce and set them aside.

6 Stir the halibut or scrod, shrimp, scallops and pepper into the sauce. Bring to a boil; reduce heat and simmer for 4 to 5 minutes more. Discard the bay leaf.

7 To serve, place the cooked clams (still in their shells) in shallow bowls. Ladle the stew mixture on top and garnish with parsley.

TIPS FROM OUR KITCHEN

To clean clams: Use a stiff brush to scrub the clams under cold running water. In an 8-quart Dutch oven, combine 4 quarts *cold water* and ⅓ cup *salt*. Add the clams and soak for 15 minutes. Drain and rinse. Discard the water. Repeat twice.

The red wine will change the color of the seafood. For a lighter wine flavor, use 1 cup wine and 1 cup broth instead of the 2 cups wine. Or, eliminate all of the wine and substitute broth for the entire amount.

Nutrition Analysis (*Per Serving*): Calories: 280 / Cholesterol: 93 mg / Carbohydrates: 14 g / Protein: 37 g / Sodium: 449 mg / Fat: 6 g (Saturated Fat: 1 g) / Potassium: 1154 mg.

CIOPPINO

BOB BURNS'S BOUILLABAISSE

BOB BURNS'S BOUILLABAISSE

Makes 8 Servings

¼ cup olive oil
2 cups chopped celery
1 cup chopped onion
1 leek, chopped (⅔ cup)
2 cloves garlic, minced
2 16-ounce cans tomatoes, cut up
1 cup dry white wine
1 bay leaf
2 tablespoons snipped parsley
½ teaspoon dried thyme, crushed
½ teaspoon fennel seed, crushed
¼ teaspoon black pepper
⅛ teaspoon powdered saffron
1 pound fresh *or* frozen flounder fillets, thawed and cut into 1-inch pieces
1 pound fresh *or* frozen haddock fillets, thawed and cut into 1-inch pieces
12 fresh *or* frozen scallops, thawed (halve any large scallops)
12 medium fresh *or* frozen peeled and deveined shrimp, thawed
1 8-ounce can clams
1 10-ounce can oysters, drained

◆　◆　◆

John Monahan
Flavors of Cape Henlopen
Village Improvement Association
Rehoboth Beach
DELAWARE

1 In a large kettle, heat the olive oil. Add the celery, onion, leek and garlic. Cook and stir for 5 minutes or until the vegetables are tender.

2 Stir in the *undrained* tomatoes, white wine, bay leaf, parsley, thyme, fennel seed, black pepper and saffron. Bring to a boil. Reduce heat and simmer, covered, for 15 minutes.

3 Add the flounder, haddock, scallops, shrimp, undrained clams and oysters. Return to a boil. Reduce heat and simmer, covered, about 5 minutes more or until the seafood is done.

 TIPS FROM OUR KITCHEN

You may notice that no salt is added to this recipe. It's a full-flavored soup that doesn't require additional salt.

If you prefer a soup with fewer solids, use only 1 pound of flounder and/or haddock.

Sea scallops are the largest type of scallop available in the United States. Bay scallops and calico scallops are smaller. Look for fresh scallops that are firm and free of excess cloudy liquid. They should be sweet smelling; spoiled scallops have a strong sulfur odor. Refrigerate scallops in their own liquid in a closed container and use within 2 days.

If you are using fresh shrimp in shells, here's how to remove the shells and devein them. Open each shell lengthwise down the body. Hold the shrimp in one hand and carefully peel back the shell starting with the head end. Leave the last section of the shell and tail intact. Either cut off the body portion of the shell, leaving the tail shell in place, or gently pull on the tail portion of the shell and remove the entire shell. To remove the vein, make a shallow slit with a sharp knife along the back of the shrimp. Use the tip of the knife to scrape out the black vein.

When cooked to doneness, the fish and scallops should become opaque, white and tender; the shrimp will be pink.

Nutrition Analysis (*Per Serving*): Calories: 282 / Cholesterol: 139 mg / Carbohydrates: 12 g / Protein: 32 g / Sodium: 467 mg / Fat: 10 g (Saturated Fat: 1 g) / Potassium: 936 mg.

MANHATTAN CLAM CHOWDER

Makes 6 Servings

- 2 cups chicken stock *or* broth
- 1 cup cubed potatoes
- ½ cup cubed carrots
- ½ cup cubed celery
- ½ cup cubed onions
- ½ teaspoon minced garlic
- ½ teaspoon snipped parsley
- ¼ teaspoon dried thyme, crushed
- ¼ teaspoon dried oregano, crushed
- 3 cups chopped, canned *or* fresh clams, with juice
- 1 cup peeled and chopped fresh tomatoes
- 1 8-ounce can tomato sauce
- 1 tablespoon butter *or* margarine
- 1 tablespoon olive oil

◆ ◆ ◆

Jerry Cegla, Executive Chef at the Edina Country Club Restaurant, told us that this chowder has been served in the restaurant for years. Although some chefs are protective about sharing recipes, Jerry said, "everyone can make soup from the same recipe and each one will come out a bit different. People will make little changes—it's just human nature."

Jerry Cegla, CFBE
Edina Country Club Restaurant
The Global Gourmet
Concordia Language Villages
Moorhead
MINNESOTA

1 In a large saucepan, stir together the chicken stock or broth, potatoes, carrots, celery, onions, thyme, garlic, parsley, and oregano. Bring to a boil. Reduce heat; cover and cook about 20 minutes or until the vegetables are tender.

2 Stir in the *undrained* clams, tomatoes, tomato sauce, butter or margarine and olive oil. Season to taste with *salt* and *pepper*. Heat until the soup is bubbly.

 TIPS FROM OUR KITCHEN

If you're using canned clams, you'll need approximately four 6½-ounce cans. For 3 cups chopped fresh clams, you'll need to buy 2 pints of shucked clams or about 36 clams in their shells. When buying shucked clams, look for plump ones with clear juices and no pieces of shell.

To clean and shuck the clams: Use a stiff brush to scrub the shells under cold running water. Then, soak the clams in salted water. To open the shells, hold the clam with the hinged

back side against a heavy cloth in the palm of your hand. Working over a plate to catch the juices, insert a sturdy, blunt-tipped knife between the shell halves. Hold the shell firmly and move the knife blade around the clam to cut the muscles that hold the shell together. Slightly twist the knife to pry open the shell. Cut the clam muscle free from the shell.

Cubed vegetables are all similar in size. To simplify cubing the vegetables: Cut the vegetables into strips that are ⅛ to ¼ inch wide. Line up and stack the strips and cut lengthwise and crosswise through the stack to make even size pieces.

Nutrition Analysis (*Per Serving*): Calories: 155 / Cholesterol: 82 mg / Carbohydrates: 15 g / Protein: 13 g / Sodium: 614 mg / Fat: 6 g (Saturated Fat: 2 g) / Potassium: 616 mg.

Manhattan Clam Chowder

FLORIDA FISH CHOWDER

FLORIDA FISH CHOWDER

Makes 4 Servings
- 1   pound fresh *or* frozen fish fillets
- ¼   cup chopped bacon *or* salt pork (2 strips)
- ½   cup chopped onion
- 2   cups water
- 1   cup diced potato
- ¾   cup diced carrot
- ½   cup chopped celery
- 2   teaspoons Worcestershire sauce
- 1   teaspoon salt
- ¼   teaspoon dried thyme, crushed
- 1   16-ounce can tomatoes, cut up
- ¼   cup catsup
- Snipped fresh parsley

♦   ♦   ♦

Helen Jackson told us that she often makes soups and chowders from scratch, just adding ingredients and tasting as she goes along. When she made this dish, she wanted just a combination of fish, celery and potatoes, but as she added ingredients, it tasted better and better after each new ingredient.

Helen Jackson
A.H.A. Breadwinners
Atlanta Housing Authority
Atlanta
GEORGIA

1 Thaw the fish, if frozen. If necessary, remove the skin from the fish fillets. Cut the fillets into 1-inch pieces; set aside.

2 In a 2-quart saucepan over medium heat, cook the bacon or salt pork until nearly crisp. Add the onion and cook just until tender. Carefully stir in the water (the mixture may splatter), potato, carrot, celery, Worcestershire sauce, salt and thyme. Bring the mixture to a boil. Reduce heat; cover and simmer about 15 minutes or until the vegetables are tender.

3 Stir in the *undrained* tomatoes and catsup; return the mixture to a boil. Reduce heat and add the reserved fish pieces to the mixture. Cover and simmer about 5 minutes or until the fish flakes easily when tested with a fork. Sprinkle the chowder with the snipped parsley before serving.

TIPS FROM OUR KITCHEN

Use a white fish such as orange roughy, haddock or cod.

Fresh fish is very perishable. If you can't cook the fish the same day you buy it, wrap it carefully in moisture- and vapor-proof material, and store it in the coldest part of the refrigerator up to 2 days.

If the fish is frozen, do not thaw it at room temperature because the outer surface will get warmer faster than the interior, which could lead to spoilage. Instead, thaw the unopened package in a container in the refrigerator overnight.

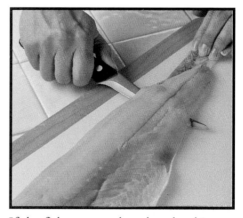

If the fish you purchase has the skin on it, use a sharp knife and carefully cut the skin from the flesh of the fish.

The tomatoes are added after the other vegetables because they take less time to cook and because the acid in tomatoes would tend to prevent the other vegetables from becoming tender.

Nutrition Analysis (*Per Serving*): Calories: 203 / Cholesterol: 46 mg / Carbohydrates: 24 g / Protein: 22 g / Sodium: 1104 mg / Fat: 3 g (Saturated Fat: 1 g) / Potassium: 863 mg.

MILDRED KEMP'S SECRET INGREDIENT CRAB SOUP

Makes 4 Servings

  4 medium tomatoes, peeled and
     chopped
  1 large green sweet pepper,
     chopped
  1 small onion, finely chopped
  1 teaspoon dry mustard
 12 ounces cooked crabmeat
  1 tablespoon margarine *or* butter
  1 tablespoon all-purpose flour
 ¼ teaspoon sugar
 ¼ teaspoon Worcestershire sauce
  2 cups milk
  1 cup half-and-half *or* light cream

◆   ◆   ◆

The Wades Point Farm is famous for its hospitality and cuisine, and guests return year after year to enjoy the ambiance of the charming inn. One of the house specialties is the crab soup that had an ingredient no one could quite figure out—and the cook would not divulge the secret. After asking several times, Inn Keeper Mildred Kemp hid in the kitchen to watch the cook prepare the soup and to discover the secret...sugar!

Mildred Kemp
From a Lighthouse Window
Chesapeake Bay Maritime
Museum
St. Michaels
MARYLAND

1 In a medium saucepan, stir together the tomatoes, green sweet pepper, onion, 2 tablespoons *water* and the dry mustard. Bring to a boil; simmer, uncovered, for 15 to 18 minutes or until the vegetables are tender. Remove from heat. Stir in the crabmeat, ¼ teaspoon *salt* and ⅛ teaspoon *pepper;* set aside.

2 In a large saucepan over medium heat, melt the margarine or butter. Stir in the flour, sugar and Worcestershire sauce. Add the milk and half-and-half or light cream all at once. Cook and stir over medium heat until the mixture is slightly thickened and bubbly. Cook and stir for 1 minute more.

3 Stir the crabmeat-vegetable mixture into the milk mixture. Heat through but *do not boil.*

◆―――◆

 TIPS FROM OUR KITCHEN

You'll need 2 to 2¼ pounds of crab legs for 12 ounces of crabmeat. To boil live crabs: In a 12- to 16-quart kettle, bring 8 quarts *water* and 2 teaspoons *salt* to a boil. Add the crabs and return the water to a boil. Reduce heat; cover and simmer for 15 minutes. Drain the crabs and refrigerate, or rinse the crabs under cold running water until they are cool enough to handle.

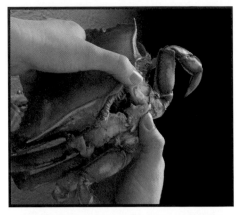

To crack a cooked crab: Turn the crab on its back. Use your thumb to pry up the tail flap or apron; twist it off and discard. Hold the crab with the top shell in one hand and grasp the bottom shell at the point where the apron was removed. Pull the top shell away from the body of the crab and discard. Use a small knife to remove the "devil's fingers" (spongy gills) from each side of the top of the crab. Discard the internal organs, mouth and small appendages at the front of the crab. To remove the meat, twist off the legs and claws using your fingers. Use a nutcracker to crack each joint, then pick out the meat. Break the body in half and remove the remaining meat.

Nutrition Analysis (*Per Serving*): Calories: 307 / Cholesterol: 104 mg / Carbohydrates: 22 g / Protein: 26 g / Sodium: 424 mg / Fat: 13 g (Saturated Fat: 6 g) / Potassium: 1066 mg.

MILDRED KEMP'S SECRET INGREDIENT CRAB SOUP

SCALLOP CHOWDER

SCALLOP CHOWDER

Makes 8 Main-Dish Servings

- 4 medium potatoes, chopped (4 cups)
- 3 cups chicken broth
- 2 stalks celery, chopped (1 cup)
- 2 carrots, chopped (1 cup)
- 1 onion, chopped (½ cup)
- 1 bay leaf
- ½ teaspoon salt
- ½ teaspoon dried thyme, crushed
- ¼ teaspoon freshly ground pepper
- 8 ounces fresh mushrooms, sliced
- ¼ cup butter *or* margarine
- 1½ pounds fresh scallops
- 1 cup dry white wine
- 1½ cups half-and-half *or* light cream

Snipped fresh chives *or* parsley
Paprika

◆   ◆   ◆

Victoria Takagi loves all aspects of cooking and entertaining. She told us that she often finds recipes and alters them to suit her own tastes. And Victoria also takes pleasure in setting the table and preparing for her guests.

Victoria Takagi
Kitchen Harmony
The Mid-Columbia Symphony
Guild
Richland
WASHINGTON

1 In a large Dutch oven, stir together the potatoes, chicken broth, celery, carrots and onion. Bring the mixture to a boil. Add the bay leaf, salt, thyme and pepper. Reduce heat; cover and simmer for 20 to 25 minutes or until the vegetables are tender. Let the mixture cool slightly and remove the bay leaf.

2 In a blender container or food processor bowl, blend or process *half* of the vegetable mixture at a time until almost smooth. Pour the pureed vegetable mixture back into the Dutch oven.

3 In a small skillet, cook the mushrooms in the butter or margarine for 4 to 5 minutes or until the mushrooms are tender. Add the scallops and white wine and cook for 2 to 3 minutes or until the scallops are opaque. Stir in the half-and-half or light cream.

4 Pour the scallop mixture into the pureed vegetable mixture and stir until well combined. Gently cook until the chowder is heated through. Sprinkle the chives or parsley and paprika over the chowder.

 TIPS FROM OUR KITCHEN

You can use either bay scallops or sea scallops in this recipe. Halve or quarter any scallops that are too large.

Fresh scallops should be firm, free of excess cloudy liquid and have a slightly sweet odor. Cover and refrigerate fresh scallops in their own liquid in a closed container and use them within 2 days.

Common white, cream and brown mushrooms all work well in this recipe. Or, try dried mushrooms that have been soaked in enough warm water to cover for 30 minutes. Rinse the mushrooms well and squeeze them to drain thoroughly. Remove and discard the tough stems.

If you prefer, 1 cup of chicken broth can be used instead of the wine.

Nutrition Analysis (*Per Serving*): Calories: 290 / Cholesterol: 56 mg / Carbohydrates: 25 g / Protein: 17 g / Sodium: 669 mg / Fat: 12 g (Saturated Fat: 7 g) / Potassium: 938 mg.

GINGER SCALLOPS

Makes 4 to 6 Servings

5	tablespoons butter *or* margarine
⅓	cup finely chopped scallions *or* green onion
1½	cups julienne-cut carrots
½	cup dry white wine
1	tablespoon grated fresh gingerroot
¾	cup heavy whipping cream
¼	teaspoon salt
¼ to ½	teaspoon freshly ground pepper
1	pound bay *or* sea scallops

✦   ✦   ✦

Food has always played an important role in Hawaiian tradition and custom, and feasting has often served both a religious and social function. As people of different nationalities arrived in Hawaii, they brought with them new crops and new methods of preparing foods which contributed to the developing culinary history of the islands. This recipe for Ginger Scallops provides us with an opportunity to sample the rich heritage of The Aloha State.

<u>*A Taste of Aloha*</u>
The Junior League of Honolulu
Honolulu
HAWAII

1 In a large skillet, melt *3 tablespoons* of the butter or margarine. Add the scallions or green onion; cook and stir for 1 minute. Add the carrots and cook for 2 minutes. Stir in the wine and gingerroot. When the mixture is thoroughly heated, add the cream, salt and pepper.

2 Cook and stir the sauce over medium-high heat about 5 minutes or until it is reduced by half.

3 Add the scallops to the sauce. Cook for 1 minute if using bay scallops or for 2 minutes if using sea scallops.

4 Stir in the remaining butter or margarine and serve.

 TIPS FROM OUR KITCHEN

Serve this creamy dish over rice or in puff pastry shells.

If you're watching calories and fat, omit the 2 tablespoons of butter that are added to the sauce just before serving.

When choosing fresh gingerroot, select a piece that's firm and heavy; avoid shriveled stems. For short-term storage of fresh gingerroot, wrap the root in a paper towel and refrigerate. For long-term storage, immerse peeled slices of gingerroot in dry sherry, wine or oil and refrigerate in a covered container for up to three months. (The ginger-flavored sherry, wine or oil can be used in cooking.) Or, place the root in a moisture and vaporproof bag and freeze. Then, grate or cut off what you need from the unpeeled frozen root.

Nutrition Analysis *(Per Serving)*: Calories: 466 / Cholesterol: 167 mg / Carbohydrates: 9 g / Protein: 31 g / Sodium: 668 mg / Fat: 33 g (Saturated Fat: 19 g) / Potassium: 796 mg.

GINGER SCALLOPS

Tuna-Noodle Casserole

TUNA-NOODLE CASSEROLE

Makes 6 Servings

4	ounces medium noodles (3 cups)
1	6½-ounce can tuna, drained and flaked
1	cup sliced celery
½	cup mayonnaise *or* salad dressing
⅓	cup chopped onion
¼	cup chopped green sweet pepper
¼	cup chopped pimiento
1	10¾-ounce can condensed cream of celery soup
½	cup milk
1	cup shredded American cheese (4 ounces)

❖   ❖   ❖

Betty Reese told us that when her children were living at home, Tuna-Noodle Casserole was a favorite. To this day, she continues to make it fairly often. She's had the recipe for at least 10 years and says it's absolutely delicious. Although Betty usually follows the recipe, she suggests that you use your best judgment and experiment with the ingredients to suit your own tastes.

Betty Reese
Dinner by Design
Everywoman's Resource Center
Topeka
KANSAS

1 Cook the noodles according to the package directions; drain and set aside. Preheat the oven to 425°.

2 In a large bowl, stir together the noodles, tuna, celery, mayonnaise or salad dressing, onion, green sweet pepper and pimiento; set aside.

3 In a medium saucepan, stir together the undiluted cream of celery soup and milk; heat through. Add the American cheese; cook and stir the mixture until the cheese melts. Add the soup mixture to the noodle mixture and gently stir to mix all of the ingredients together.

4 Spoon the tuna-noodle mixture into a 2-quart casserole dish. Cover and bake in the 425° oven for 20 to 30 minutes or until the casserole is heated through.

TIPS FROM OUR KITCHEN

Chunk-style tuna (top right) is the most common and is priced somewhere between the solid and flaked varieties.

If you prefer the vegetables to be a little less crunchy, cook them with the noodles in the boiling water. Or, cook the vegetables separately in 1 tablespoon *margarine* or *butter* until the vegetables are tender.

Try adding a topping to the casserole: In a small bowl, stir together ½ cup *soft bread crumbs*, 2 tablespoons *wheat germ* and 1 tablespoon melted *margarine* or *butter*. Sprinkle the mixture over the casserole and bake as above, removing the cover from the dish for the last few minutes of cooking.

To make soft bread crumbs: Place 1 slice of torn bread in a food processing bowl. Cover and process until small crumbs form.

Canned tuna is available either packed in oil or water. Solid-pack tuna (top left) is the most expensive and flaked or grated tuna (bottom) is the least expensive.

Nutrition Analysis (*Per Serving*): Calories: 523 / Cholesterol: 69 mg / Carbohydrates: 21 g / Protein: 18 g / Sodium: 1018 mg / Fat: 42 g (Saturated Fat: 9 g) / Potassium: 325 mg.

DEEP DISH SALMON PIE

Makes 4 to 6 Servings

Creamed Salmon:
- 3 tablespoons butter *or* margarine
- 2 small onions, chopped (⅔ cup)
- 1 medium green sweet pepper, chopped (¾ cup)
- 5 tablespoons all-purpose flour
- ½ teaspoon salt
- 2⅔ cups milk
- 1 14¾-ounce can salmon, drained, flaked and skin and bones removed
- 1 tablespoon lemon juice

Cheese Rolls:
- 1½ cups all-purpose flour
- 1 tablespoon baking powder
- ½ teaspoon salt
- 3 tablespoons shortening
- ½ cup milk *or* water
- ¾ cup shredded cheddar, mozzarella, Swiss, American *or* hot pepper cheese (3 ounces)
- ¼ cup chopped pimiento (optional)

◆   ◆   ◆

The recipes in this wonderful cookbook were contributed by the staff, board members and volunteers of the center.

Sue M. Young
Novato Human Needs Center Cookbook
Novato Human Needs Center
Novato
CALIFORNIA

1 Preheat the oven to 425°. Grease a 2-quart baking dish. Set aside.

2 To make the Creamed Salmon: In a saucepan, melt the butter or margarine. Add the onion and green sweet pepper to the saucepan; cook until the vegetables are tender. Stir in the flour and the ½ teaspoon salt. Slowly add the 2⅔ cups milk. Cook and stir until the mixture is thickened and bubbly. Stir in the salmon and lemon juice. Pour the mixture into the prepared baking dish.

3 To make the Cheese Rolls: In a medium bowl, mix together the flour, baking powder and the ½ teaspoon salt. Using a pastry blender, cut in the shortening. Add the ½ cup milk or water. Stir just until the dough clings together.

4 Turn the dough out onto a lightly floured surface. Knead the dough gently for 10 to 12 strokes. Roll the dough out to a 12x8-inch rectangle. Sprinkle the cheese and pimiento (if using) over the dough. Roll up from a long side.

5 Cut into 8 slices. Using a rolling pin or your hand, slightly flatten the slices. Place the spirals on top of the salmon mixture.

6 Bake the casserole in the 425° oven about 25 minutes or until brown. Let stand for 10 minutes before serving.

 TIPS FROM OUR KITCHEN

If desired, substitute two 6½- or 7-ounce cans of tuna for the salmon.

If you use milk instead of water in these rolls, they will be more tender.

This casserole is very hot when it first comes out of the oven. So before serving, be sure to let it stand for the full 10 minutes specified in the recipe.

Nutrition Analysis (*Per Serving*): Calories: 679 / Cholesterol: 90 mg / Carbohydrates: 57 g / Protein: 40 g / Sodium: 1339 mg / Fat: 32 g (Saturated Fat: 14 g) / Potassium: 845 mg.

DEEP DISH SALMON PIE

TUNA FISH SOUFFLÉ

TUNA FISH SOUFFLÉ

Makes 4 Servings

1½ cups soft bread crumbs
    (2 slices)
1   6½- or 7-ounce can water-
    packed tuna, drained and
    flaked
1   teaspoon lemon juice
½   teaspoon paprika
¾   cup milk
3   egg yolks, beaten
3   egg whites
Paprika (optional)

◆   ◆   ◆

In order to raise funds for needed church renovations, the Adult Fellowship class from the Good Shepherd's United Church of Christ worked together to create Good Shepherd's Favorite Recipes. *Contributions were requested from friends and members "willing to share recipes and helpful hints." Dot Fleming answered the call with her family favorite, Tuna Fish Soufflé.*

Dot Fleming
Good Shepherd's Favorite Recipes
Good Shepherd's United Church of Christ
Boyertown
PENNSYLVANIA

1 Preheat the oven to 350°. Grease a 1- to 1½-quart baking dish. Set aside.

2 In a large bowl, combine the bread crumbs, tuna, lemon juice and the ½ teaspoon paprika; set aside.

3 In a small saucepan, heat the milk until it is very warm. Pour the warm milk over the bread crumb mixture. Stir in the egg yolks.

4 In a clean, large bowl, beat the egg whites using an electric mixer until stiff peaks form. Gently fold the beaten egg whites into the bread crumb mixture.

5 Carefully transfer the mixture into the prepared baking dish. If desired, sprinkle with paprika. Set the baking dish in a 13x9x2-inch pan and add hot water to the pan to a 1-inch depth.

6 Bake in the 350° oven about 30 minutes or until a knife inserted near the center comes out clean.

 TIPS FROM OUR KITCHEN

This recipe also works well with canned salmon.

Two slices of bread will give you the right amount of soft bread crumbs. Tear the bread by hand into small pieces. Or, tear the bread into pieces and place in a blender container or a food processor work bowl with a steel blade. Blend or process until coarsely chopped.

Setting the baking dish in a pan of water during baking eliminates the potential problem of overcooking or curdling the eggs.

Cheese sauce or creamed peas are perfect accompaniments to this dish.

Nutrition Analysis (*Per Serving*): Calories: 188 / Cholesterol: 182 mg / Carbohydrates: 11 g / Protein: 20 g / Sodium: 337 mg / Fat: 6 g (Saturated Fat: 2 g) / Potassium: 273 mg.

ARTICHOKE AND SHRIMP CASSEROLE

Makes 4 Servings

1 9-ounce package frozen
   artichoke hearts
1 teaspoon salt
12 ounces fresh *or* frozen
   peeled and deveined shrimp
1½ cups sliced fresh mushrooms
4 tablespoons butter *or*
   margarine
1 8-ounce can sliced water
   chestnuts, drained
2 tablespoons all-purpose
   flour
1¼ cups milk
2 tablespoons dry sherry
1 teaspoon Worcestershire
   sauce
¼ teaspoon salt
⅛ teaspoon pepper
¼ cup grated Parmesan cheese
Dash paprika

◆ ◆ ◆

Barbara Wiedner, founder of
Grandmothers for Peace, told us
that the organization's purpose is
to develop a society that enables
children to "grow up as healthy,
productive citizens." Founded
eleven years ago, the organiza-
tion has expanded internation-
ally "through word of mouth."

Marjorie Welsch
Grandmothers for Peace
Cherished Recipes
Grandmothers for Peace
Sacramento
CALIFORNIA

1 Preheat the oven to 375°.

2 Cook the artichoke hearts according to the package directions; drain well. Cut any large artichokes in half. Place the artichoke hearts in a 1½-quart casserole dish.

3 Bring 1 quart *water* and the 1 teaspoon salt to a boil. Add the shrimp and bring to a second boil. Cook for 1 to 3 minutes or until the shrimp turn pink, stirring occasionally. Remove from heat and immediately rinse the shrimp under cold, running water. Drain well and arrange over the artichoke hearts.

4 In a medium saucepan over medium heat, cook and stir the mushrooms in *2 tablespoons* of the butter or margarine until tender. Pour the mushroom mixture over the shrimp. Sprinkle with the water chestnuts.

5 In the same saucepan, melt the remaining butter or margarine. Stir in the flour. Add the milk all at once. Cook and stir over medium heat until the mixture is thickened and bubbly. Cook and stir for 1 minute more.

6 Stir in the sherry, Worcestershire sauce, the ¼ teaspoon salt and the pepper. Pour the sauce over the water chestnuts. Sprinkle the Parmesan cheese and paprika over the top. Bake in the 375° oven for 20 to 25 minutes or until heated through.

 TIPS FROM OUR KITCHEN

If using fresh shrimp in shells, here's how to remove the shell. Using your fingers, open the shell lengthwise down the body. Hold the shrimp in one hand and carefully peel back the shell starting with the head end. Leave the last section of the shell and tail intact. Either cut the body portion of the shell off, leaving the tail shell in place, or gently pull on the tail portion of the shell and remove the entire shell. To remove the vein, make a shallow slit with a sharp knife along the back of the shrimp. Use the tip of the knife to scrape out the black vein.

For variety, add ½ teaspoon dried basil or thyme to the sauce before pouring it over the water chestnuts.

If you wish, bake this recipe in individual casseroles. Or, serve the baked casserole mixture in patty shells that have been baked according to package directions.

Nutrition Analysis: (*Per Serving*): Calories: 323 / Cholesterol: 172 mg / Carbohydrates: 23 g / Protein: 24 g / Sodium: 783 mg / Fat: 16 g (Saturated Fat: 9 g) / Potassium: 706 mg.

ARTICHOKE AND SHRIMP CASSEROLE

SIMPLE SHRIMP CREOLE

SIMPLE SHRIMP CREOLE

Makes 4 Servings

2 tablespoons butter *or* margarine
½ cup finely chopped onion
2 tablespoons all-purpose flour
3 cups water
1 6-ounce can tomato paste
½ cup finely chopped green sweet pepper
¼ cup finely chopped celery
1 teaspoon snipped parsley
½ teaspoon salt
¼ teaspoon bottled hot pepper sauce
Dash to ⅛ teaspoon ground red pepper
1 bay leaf
2 cups cooked shrimp
2 cups hot cooked rice

♦ ♦ ♦

After the parishoners of All Saints' Episcopal Church found themselves buying mimeographed copies of the recipes from a fund-raising dinner in 1974, they began to put together this wonderful cookbook.

La Bonne Cuisine: Cooking New Orleans Style
The Women of All Saints' Episcopal Church
New Orleans
LOUISIANA

1 In a large heavy skillet over medium heat, melt the butter or margarine. Add the onion and cook until tender but not brown.

2 Stir in the flour. Add the water, tomato paste, green pepper, celery, parsley, salt, hot pepper sauce, ground red pepper and bay leaf.

3 Cook, uncovered, over medium-low heat about 30 minutes or until thickened, stirring occasionally.

4 Stir in the shrimp and heat through. Remove the bay leaf. Serve over the hot cooked rice.

TIPS FROM OUR KITCHEN

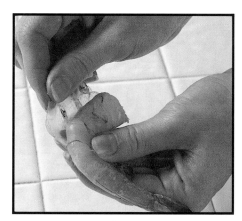

To remove shells from fresh shrimp: Open the shell lengthwise down the body. Remove the legs. Hold the shrimp in one hand and carefully peel back the shell starting with the head end. Leave the last section of the shell and tail intact.

Either cut the body portion of the shell off, leaving the tail shell in place, or gently pull on the tail portion of the shell to remove the entire shell.

To devein shrimp: Make a shallow slit with a sharp knife along the back of the shrimp. Use the tip of the knife to scrape out the black vein.

To cook raw, shelled shrimp: In a large saucepan, heat 6 cups *water* and 2 tablespoons *salt* to boiling. Add the shelled shrimp. Reduce the heat and simmer for 1 to 3 minutes or until the shrimp turns pink. Drain.

Breaded fried okra makes a perfect accompaniment to this dish.

Nutrition Analysis *(Per Serving)*: Calories: 324 / Cholesterol: 163 mg / Carbohydrates: 44 g / Protein: 21 g / Sodium: 542 mg / Fat: 7 g (Saturated Fat: 4 g) Potassium: 715 mg.

recipe index

T - Z

Metric Cooking Hints

By making a few conversions, cooks in Australia, Canada, and the United Kingdom can use the recipes in Better Homes and Gardens ® Casual Suppers with confidence. The charts on this page provide a guide for converting measurements from the U.S. customary system, which is used throughout this book, to the imperial and metric systems. There also is a conversion table for oven temperatures to accommodate the differences in oven calibrations.

Volume and Weight: Americans traditionally use cup measures for liquid and solid ingredients. The chart (top right) shows the approximate imperial and metric equivalents. If you are accustomed to weighing solid ingredients, here are some helpful approximate equivalents.
■ 1 cup butter, caster sugar, or rice = 8 ounces = about 250 grams
■ 1 cup flour = 4 ounces = about 125 grams
■ 1 cup icing sugar = 5 ounces = about 150 grams
   Spoon measures are used for smaller amounts of ingredients. Although the size of the tablespoon varies slightly among countries. However, for practical purposes and for recipes in this book, a straight substitution is all that's necessary.
   Measurements made using cups or spoons should always be level, unless stated otherwise.

Product Differences: Most of the ingredients called for in the recipes in this book are available in English-speaking countries. However, some are known by different names. Here are some common American ingredients and their possible counterparts:
■ Sugar is granulated or caster sugar.
■ Powdered sugar is icing sugar.
■ All-purpose flour is plain household flour or white flour. When self-rising flour is used in place of all-purpose flour in a recipe that calls for leavening, omit the leavening agent (baking soda or baking powder) and salt.
■ Light corn syrup is golden syrup.
■ Cornstarch is cornflour.
■ Baking soda is bicarbonate of soda.
■ Vanilla is vanilla essence.

Useful Equivalents

⅛ teaspoon = 0.5ml	⅔ cup = 5 fluid ounces = 150ml
¼ teaspoon = 1ml	¾ cup = 6 fluid ounces = 175ml
½ teaspoon = 2 ml	1 cup = 8 fluid ounces = 250ml
1 teaspoon = 5 ml	2 cups = 1 pint
¼ cup = 2 fluid ounces = 50ml	2 pints = 1 litre
⅓ cup = 3 fluid ounces = 75ml	½ inch =1 centimetre
½ cup = 4 fluid ounces = 125ml	1 inch = 2 centimetres

Baking Pan Sizes

American	Metric
8x1½-inch round baking pan	20x4-centimetre sandwich or cake tin
9x1½-inch round baking pan	23x3.5-centimetre sandwich or cake tin
11x7x1½-inch baking pan	28x18x4-centimetre baking pan
13x9x2-inch baking pan	32.5x23x5-centimetre baking pan
12x7½x2-inch baking dish	30x19x5-centimetre baking pan
15x10x1-inch baking pan	38x25.5x2.5-centimetre baking pan (Swiss roll tin)
9-inch pie plate	22x4- or 23x4-centimetre pie plate
7- or 8-inch springform pan	18- or 20-centimetre springform or loose-bottom cake tin
9x5x3-inch loaf pan	23x13x6-centimetre or 2-pound narrow loaf pan or paté tin
1½-quart casserole	1.5-litre casserole
2-quart casserole	2-litre casserole

Oven Temperature Equivalents

Farenheit Setting	Celsius Setting*	Gas Setting
300°F	150°C	Gas Mark 2
325°F	160°C	Gas Mark 3
350°F	180°C	Gas Mark 4
375°F	190°C	Gas Mark 5
400°F	200°C	Gas Mark 6
425°F	220°C	Gas Mark 7
450°F	230°C	Gas Mark 8
Broil		Grill

*Electric and gas ovens may be calibrated using Celsius. However, increase the Celsius setting 10 to 20 degrees when cooking above 160°C with an electric oven. For convection or forced-air ovens (gas or electric), lower the temperature setting 10°C when cooking at all heat levels.